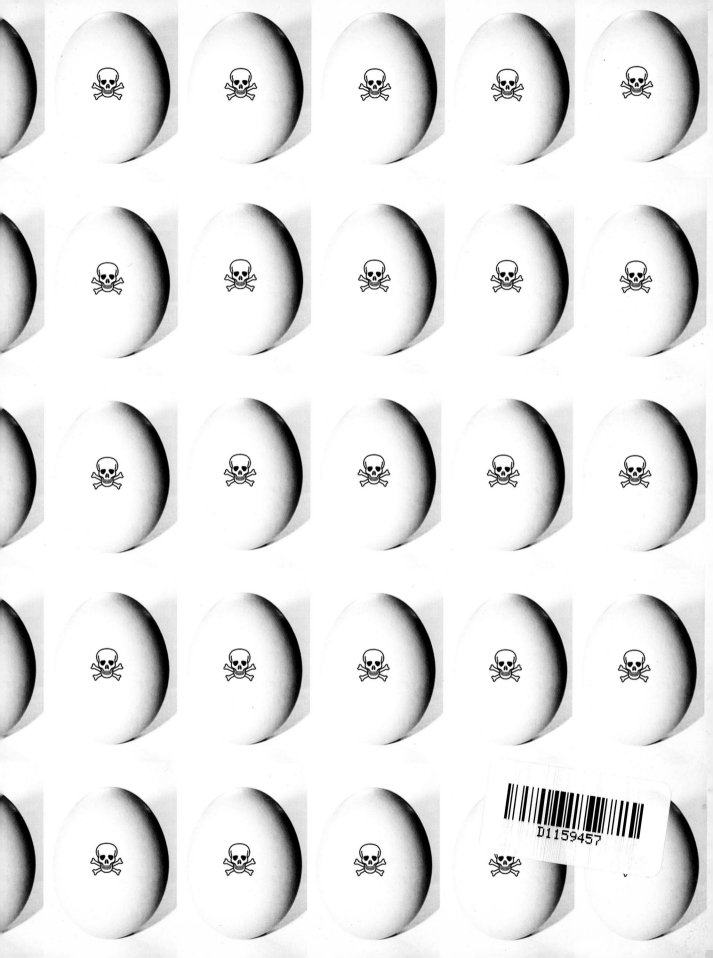

CRUEL

CRUEL

BEARING WITNESS TO
ANIMAL EXPLOITATION

Sue Coe

with notes by Judy Brody

OR Books

New York • London

Published by OR Books, New York and London
Visit our website at www.orbooks.com

First printing 2012

Cataloging-in-Publication data is available from the Library of Congress
A catalog record for this book is available from the British Library

Typeset and designed by Courtney Andujar

Printed by BookMobile in Canada. The printer is 100% wind-powered.

ISBN 978-1-935928-72-0 paperback
ISBN 978-1-935928-73-7 e-book
ISBN 978-1-935928-74-4 hardcover

TABLE OF CONTENTS

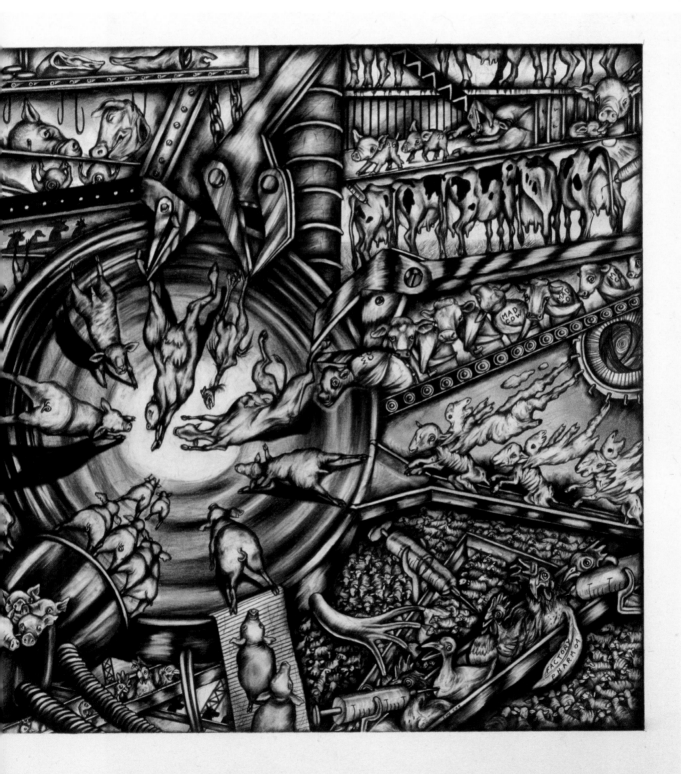

Weapon of Mass Destruction - Factory Farming   Sue Coe '03

COUNTY FAIR

One week long, the County Fair is a venue for farmers to sell their prize animals. An event of Americana, signaling the end of summer. This year, the tiny, winding country road leading up to the fair was covered in Tea Party posters and slogans. They were carefully covered in plastic sheeting to protect them from any rain showers. I am approached by a woman with a clipboard and an offer to go to a meeting "to take our country back." At the entrance is a big sign: "No Dogs and no Alcoholic beverages," as though the combination of both those things could be the end of civilization as we know it, and then willing hands are branded with a stamp, and in we go.

All the animals are young, chained, and kept in a state of gleaming perfection, groomed and blow-dried, showered, combed and cosseted. At the end of the fair they will be auctioned off. The young cows lick each other's faces, for they are siblings, chained together—at the end of the fair they will be sold and separated forever. Animals lined up in covered stalls, with the background noise of the perpetual demolition derby and the fun fair and shooting galleries. Over the heads of the livestock will be the rosettes showing prize status: first prize or second prize, and usually a photograph of the family and how many generations they have been in business. At the fun fair will be the prizes of giant, stuffed cartoon animals, made in China, dangling by nooses, swaying in the wind as a lure for children, their acrylic fur getting dusty. Or tiny goldfish bowls, each with one isolated goldfish, some already dead, to take home.

The live animals wince at each spectacular demolition crash and at the human jeers. There is a "petting zoo" of younger animals to feed with peanuts or dried corn. In small fenced areas will be multicolored newborn piglets with a sow, newborn goats with big, plastic numbered tags as big as their heads punched into their ears, tiny baby donkeys with heads lowered. Children's hands dangle over the fences to touch soft fur. There will be the calf alone in a stall, to be auctioned to the highest bidder. He will suckle on hands and fingers. Sometimes more exotic animal prisoners will be used as a photo opportunity, a traveling zoo. $10 for a photograph with tigers as a backdrop for family groups. A tiger cub is more desirable and costs $20 for a photograph. Camels and kangaroos with their babies cower next to the shattering noise of old cars being smashed to pieces. The baby kangaroos leap back into the pouch at each sharp noise. Some of the babies are quite large, nearly as large as their mother, and they unbelievably squeeze themselves back into the pouch, diving in headfirst. The pouch bulges with lumpy shapes and goes still with the back paws sticking out at the top. Primates huddle in their cages with eyes that avoid all human gaze. I think they went insane a long time ago. Occasionally a monkey will get a wrapped candy thrown at them through the bars—and their world changes. The sweet is unwrapped slowly, with careful long fingers, and put aside— the transparent, multicolored wrapping is smoothed out and held up to one eye, rotated to view the sky in different colors.

In the winter season the fittingly biblical crèche animals will be bought from their cages, rented out to malls to stand in straw, huddled around a plastic Jesus in a manger.

The food stalls sell mystery meat products deeply fried, with melted cheese, on a soft white roll. Cotton candy and elephant ears: a giant deep-fried slab of dough covered with powdered sugar. Fried hot dogs and fried ice cream, french fries, fried anything, and gallons of soda. Food combinations that only a chef who loathes and despises the human heart can concoct.

At the larger state fairs will be sinister Army recruiting stands festooned with flags, the fair a prime hunting ground for the war on youth. There will be a large-breasted, attractive blonde female bursting out of tight military camo clothing, offering a gun to shoot a bull's eye to any young male who is interested. The young men line up for a chance to test their skills and get the woman's attention. In this world you are either a chicken or a chicken plucker, and these kids are already targeted. Over fifty percent of jobs in rural America are government jobs, the army of the unemployed.

Another display is of taxidermy, the animals stuffed, their fur threadbare patches: the black bear standing up, frozen, waiting to strike, a mountain lion permanently crouching, wild turkeys with their natural colors dulled. Trout swimming nailed to planks. Decapitated heads of deer. A dusty mink next to a leghold trap. Next to them is a recruiter for the NRA. Next to that is a miniature fish farm, promoting the profit of raising fish—a grey tank inside of which fish are crammed, swimming around a tube of oxygen.

A huge, glass refrigerated box is so strange: inside it a giant life-sized butter sculpture of a butter cow and a butter calf, on a butter meadow with butter flowers, takes form, as the sculptor shapes slabs of bright yellow butter with a palette knife. Ironically, the large dairy near the state fairgrounds is called by the locals "the concentration camp," as the cows there never leave their milking stalls, which are in long, dark sheds. They never go outside, unless it's to be trucked to slaughter, never stand on green grass with their calves. By the last day of the fair, this high-cholesterol icon of milk and butter will be completed. Where it goes later to melt, nobody knows.

There will be chainsaw sculptures that make bears appear like magic from tree trunks. More chainsaw art will be wooden lawn signs, and most this year are slogans critical of President Obama, who has the dubious honor of replacing signs about the mother-in-law and "Welcome to Our Home." The quality of the craftsmanship of the signs is as crude as the phrases.

Many of the fairgoers are morbidly obese, some so heavy that two legs can no longer hold their weight. They maneuver around the mud ruts in silent mobile carts, as if on a planet with no gravity, using the carts' fold-out table attachments to hold the fried food, which can be consumed on the go.

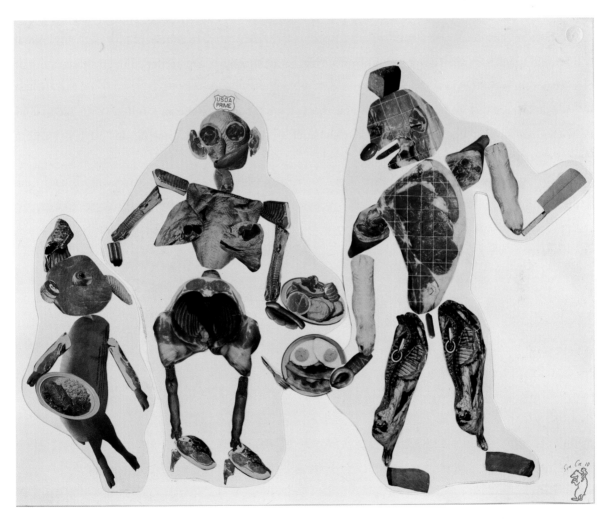

To be larger or the largest is the theme of the fairs. Anything living or dead must be judged for its giant proportions: cows, children, humans, vegetables, cakes and bread. In the usually deserted vegetable tent, giant tomatoes, potatoes, onions and squashes wait, dehydrated, on trestle tables, to be judged.

All that is normal-sized are the stretch jeans bursting at the seams, forcing flesh into manageable encased shapes resembling a human body.

The last remnants of childhood innocence are reflected in the children of farmers, who care for their 4-H club animal—they are sincere and have bonded with the animal they raised from an egg, or from birth. The cages are spotless and the name and heritage of the animal proudly displayed. The young faces of animals and humans alike are open and eager. The latter have not yet come to terms with the reality that their beloved animal will be slaughtered. When I sketch the animals, the teenager always stands by watching, fascinated by the pencil marks, willing to pose with their animal and explain anything about the breed. Adults have already developed a comfortable disconnect: they are quick to comment how tasty this animal will be, and quick to display a frozen knowing smirk that denotes they are hardened to any beseeching or pleading of their child to save the animal's life.

We do not see that we humans are simultaneously the infection and the antibodies. White blood cells destruct themselves to consume: it's a nice trick, suicide bombers of lard. Leaving this earth not with a bang but a diabetic whimper.

Foie Gras Duck- force feeding
tube sometimes punctures the throat.
Ducks brought to brink of death to expand
the liver.

Turkey chicks in confinement
begin to peck the weakest bird

Chicks for sale
at roadside stand
May

Bird at County Fair

Beautiful   Birds   Sue Coe

A farmer purchased six Holstien calves - they cost $5 each.* he tied them to a tractor and left them to die. They had lost weight from birth 80lbs to 60lbs. They were so skeletal could not stand - all had contageous diseases, seizures, sunken eyes. An ASPCA rescue officer did something - they were resued. When confronted the farmer said - "they only cost me $5, so what?"

* male dairy calves are worth almost nothing

HOPE

Our human blind spot is how we treat animals, and by extension, our only home: planet earth. This includes how we treat those accused of being animals, those who are incarcerated, and peoples of other lands that are deemed "the enemy." Ancient Rome had a term: *homo sacer*, meaning "the accursed." Accepted only as a biological entity, functioning in the realm of an animal. Those so named can be killed without penalty, by a society that despises these different forms of life. Many human beings the world over are without legal rights, especially women, children, those that are deemed a threat to the dominant order, and non-human animals. This hierarchy within a culture can only function because the very words, the language, prepare for a mental acceptance of genocide. It does not happen overnight, but can happen after months of increasing indoctrination.

The question is not why people eat meat, but why are not more people vegan? People avoid veganism in America because they are kept ignorant of different choices, the reality of how meat is created is hidden from them, and because every family celebration is linked historically to dead animals. To afford the largest turkey is to denote success—this "diet" has become the cultural icon for a family's survival. The dead animal centerpiece is surrounded by a lesser cast of vegetables.

The child who chooses an ethical diet goes against an entire family's enjoyment and convenience, and runs the risk of starting a fight or being teased and bullied at these rare moments of family unity and fun. There are many complex reasons, cultural, economic, social, religious, propaganda about meat being healthy, or meals being nutritionally incomplete without animal produce. To believe that consuming meat is enjoyable and satisfying makes the lack of it a kind of deprivation. The odor of cooking flesh, being key to family group bonding, is linked to the reality we are a highly social species. Social change, a break away from the group, is created by those who have no choice, those who do not benefit from the status quo. Our conundrum as animal advocates is that animals speak, but humans are deaf and blind to what they are saying. Animals have no choice, cannot change their fate—they are bred to be murdered by the billions every day—and are completely under human power and control.

Human beings who attempt to speak for non-human animals feel isolated from the majority of their own species that routinely exploit and kill animals. Their empathy for others is the polar opposite of power and control. This isolation is enforced economically and socially in nearly every setting where humans gather. The working poor—a strange phrase, as "to work" should bring a living wage—are the second victims of the meat industry, their life spans cut short by poor nutrition, lack of health care, lack of access to fresh fruit and vegetables and whole grains, and, if their jobs are within the "food" industry, because they work in chemical-soaked fields and inside slaughterhouses. Yet despite it all, meat consumption is dropping in the United States. Generally, more people than ever before are aware of animal suffering, and animal advocacy groups are growing in number.

The human population of the planet—seven billion—cannot continue to eat animals without factory farming those animals. It's illogical to suggest that "free range" or "humanely-produced meat" can solve this problem. It's a marketing ploy directed at the middle-class consumer that gives the illusion that there is an ethical choice for those with extra money to purchase a conscience. By the year 2050, there will be double the amount of land animals raised for food, not counting the megatons of fish fed to those same farmed animals: this is the prediction of the meat industry, who have a blood-red crystal ball; they count on our inability to change. Science and common sense suggest this will destroy the ecosystem, acidify oceans, pollute aquifers, and spread infectious disease. In the meantime, governments worldwide subsidize an industry that contributes more to global warming than any other.

The hope is transparency and daylight. Being aware of parts of the puzzle, sharing our knowledge and culture, as it fits together like a stained glass window that lets in all forms of light. In terms of the industrial herding complex, factory farming is an iron boot, crushing the female, as ninety percent of factory-farmed animals are young females. We cannot turn back time and return to a pastoral, gatherer society, but we can highlight parts of the puzzle to explain how our species got on this road.

One tap on a rock does not make it shatter. It's all those taps down the ages, over time, that break solid rock. In any social justice movement there is a profound altering of course. The more openness and transparency, the more there can be leaps in consciousness and the creation of alternative paths.

The masses accept genocide not because they are evil or cruel (although the victims certainly have justification for that thought, and some humans are cruel, most especially those cloaked in the guise of corporations where they can be faceless and unaccountable). We accept genocide because of the mundane emotion of fear and the instinct of our species to go along with the dominant social order. This, in the past, protected our species but is now creating the opposite result. To ask questions would be risking the same fate of the victim. It's always easier to look away. Out of sight, out of mind. It's mentally easier to justify cruelty and torture than to face silent collusion.

Animals do not exist for the benefit of humans. We do not exist to be food for corporations. Indoctrination allows us to disengage, diverts us from empathy and compassion (the reason our species has survived this long) and toward tolerating escalating destruction. Our actions determine our level of understanding. The unwillingness to look over that wall is socially supported and continually reinforced. The majority find this lulling mentality preferable because they are not connected to reality, just an economic machine that prompts the correct responses to survive short term.

Food has been a tool/weapon of cultural imperialism since the beginning of time. Destroying local crops, crop variety, and accumulated shared wisdom about nature, takes us from a state of independence to becoming servile, which services a dominant culture. The desire to identify and name (own) property forces the poor to be in a continuous state of war to protect corporate power. The Army is the army of the unemployed. Wars come about when there is surplus, a surplus population of humans, a mono crop. Western culture attempts to lower the reality of continuous wars into justifications for protecting property and "rights," but in this century, those "rights" have become a cloak for unregulated corporations. This happens without us comprehending that we are the property, WE ARE THE FACTORY-FARMED ANIMALS, we are the fodder, both the consumer and the consumed. Overproduction stems from inequality. There are those who labor with few or no rights, and then those that reap and control the surplus. The animal body is part of the capitalist labor process, an industry designed for the breeding of animals, including us, only to slaughter them. What was formerly an extreme right ideology is now mainstream: that the fetus has to be protected, but only up until birth, at which point that child is slotted into what makes the most profit. Ignorance creates profit, diseases make profit, wars make profit.

If our food came out of the living earth, not a patented chemical stew—if it were made visible—it would need tending. Labor is acknowledged: young men and women would not be surplus, but rather essential to feed the tribe, their energy used in partnership with nature herself. First, grain storage surplus then industrialization has created the disconnect from reality. What used to be human and animal slaves who created surplus, has now become an animal machine. We are dangerously living in complete unreality, living lives in a bubble of bogus technology with no basic survival skills other than to get into debt to continue to survive. Does a child even make a connection between "milk" and a living cow who lost her calf? Can she grow a plant? Does she see that by consuming animals, who are fed on grain, she is starving children on the other side of the world? Living in unreality, we can commit horrendous crimes against others, and be immune from immediate consequences. But wars waged do have consequences.

One vegan spares the lives of ninety-five other animals a year, and embraces a world of different tastes of healthy, real, plant-based food, tended with care from organic farms, in backyards or on rooftops—all the colors of the rainbow. Healthy for us and the planet. On the human-centric analysis alone, there is ample evidence to begin a plant-based diet and protect what habitable environment remains.

If a consumer were invited into a slaughterhouse or factory farm before she ate her burger, would she find it so palatable? If she saw the piglets having their testicles torn off by hand, saw the calves punched and beaten, saw chickens making nests on the bones and feathers of their dead cage members, would she eat the chicken or that chicken's eggs? If she saw a cow mourning her calf, that behind every glass of milk is a grieving mother who cries for days and nights to find her child, would she want to drink? If she saw animals who had never walked on grass or seen blue sky or who had only a few inches of cage space try and protect their offspring from slaughter, would her appetite be whetted? If she saw the freeborn animals poisoned and trapped and hunted so cattle could become burgers, would she still opt for that burger? Perhaps. But many others would hesitate, and start to consider alternatives.

The meat industry recognizes this: and so food animals are hidden in long steel sheds and politicians are pressured to stop hidden video and testimony of the whistle blowers. And this is why animal rights activists are accused of terrorism. It's seductive to believe that all humans are innately greedy and cruel based on how greatly animals suffer, but the meat industry does not agree. If it did, then we could openly visit factory farms and slaughterhouses. Our tasks now are to question why this is hidden, make the links, demand transparency, and provide alternatives. If cigarette packets now have coffins on them and graphic depictions of lung cancer, then shouldn't a burger's packaging depict the intestines and stomach spilling from a dying cow or a human heart clogged with fat?

As I am typing this, a cow is crying a few acres from where I live. She has cried every few seconds for the last forty-eight hours, not stopping to eat or drink. I know why: her calf has been stolen from her. Her cries must be heard for a radius of a mile, yet no one is listening. She hopes her calf will hear, know where she is, and return. She does not have the luxury of hopelessness, and neither do we.

Veal Carcass - Skinner has lost three fingers

Slaughter House Tuscon May 88 Goats before Pigs

PORKOPOLIS 66

Swift:- Butcher To The World

THE MONEY BEAST

In *The Certificate* by Isaac Bashevis Singer, the narrator stops in front of a sausage shop and addresses the sausages hanging in the window.

> *You were once alive, you suffered, but you're beyond your sorrows now. There's no trace of your writhing or suffering anywhere. Is there a memorial tablet somewhere in the cosmos on which it is written that a cow named Kvyatule allowed herself to be milked for eleven years? Then in the twelfth year, when her udder had shrunk, she was led to a slaughterhouse, where a blessing was recited over her and her throat was cut . . . Is there a paradise for the slaughtered cattle and chickens and pigs, for frogs that have been trodden underfoot, for fish that have been hooked and pulled from the sea, for the Jews whom Petlyura tortured, whom the Bolsheviks shot, for the sixty thousand soldiers who shed their blood at Verdun?*

The meat industry and the economic system in which we are suspended are attempting to rewrite human instinct, to steer profits to the few. A hierarchy of those special ones who deserve more is important to this philosophy, whether it is based on race, gender, sexual orientation, or species. Blaming the victim and divide and conquer are the weapons of power and control.

Under the cloak of "freedom" and the "free market," corporations grind life into dirt. The meat industry funds its scripted stooges to enter government to dismantle the already fragile health and safety laws that protect the public, to pillage public lands and destroy life.

Who would you save from the truck barreling down the road: the little girl running into the road or the dog? This question is a classic hypothetical false choice used by animal abusers to defend themselves. As human beings, we are capable of something called "foresight" and we are in the driver's seat. Most of us would instinctively swerve to avoid killing any species on the road if at all possible. Humans with foresight are swerving away by the millions from animal agriculture.

Social justice for animals cannot be just reduced to "consumer choice." Non-human animals are a class of beings, and their oppression is a matter of social justice. They have no power and no voice. In the last century, people became more aware of farmed animal suffering thanks to activists of all stripes. More and more, we understand that factory farms (Concentrated Animal Feeding Operations or CAFOs) are destructive to the planet, animals, and our health. Yet still governments place immediate, short-term profit before everything else. Confronting a violent industry that abuses its own employees, lies, misinforms, and purchases politicians is not easy. All we have are tiny pebbles in a truth slingshot to fight a twenty-four-hour-a-day death machine.

Ninety-nine percent of animal food production goes on behind closed doors, for obvious reasons. Most large slaughterhouses are better guarded than maximum security prisons. CAFOs need to get into the realm of political accountability, which is difficult when the government is becoming the corporation. Animals are *homo sacer*, which means they have a biological existence, but not a legal existence with concurrent rights. Owning other beings is profitable, and owning other beings leads to disrespect and abuse, both within the industry and at the consumer level. Animals are products that are disassembled. The common lie of the meat industry, repeated so many times that it has come to be accepted as the truth, is that animal producers do not abuse animals because it is not in their economic interest. If you believe that, then read no further. For those who know, no explanation is necessary; for those who do not know, no explanation is possible. There are varying levels of cruelty inflicted on farmed animals, and it is within that wiggle room (would you prefer to be waterboarded on a mattress or a wooden board?) that the industry is opportunistically marketing "happy meat," with the reluctant collusion of the consumer. The industry realized that in order to counteract the information about factory farming, to muffle the voices of a growing animal advocate population, they could extend their market by selling higher priced products labeled as "humane, free range, healthy, cage free, organic, etc.," not as an alternative, but as an addition that would appeal to the dwindling middle classes by exploiting their extra cash and concerns for their own health. If the absurd question posited is, "What is the most humane way to kill pigs?" then Temple Grandin could be correct, gassing them in CO2 chambers to stun them prior to slaughter is more humane than using a captive bolt pistol. If the question is, "Why are we murdering pigs?" then the answer is: for profit. The meat industry's statement, most often uttered by animal scientists in the indirect or direct pay of the industry—that they are feeding the hungry world by more intensive meat production—references questionable science. It's a perspective colored by money, not science. Degrees can be bought. Universities work hard at grinding out the stupid; it's another billion-dollar business. Animal agriculture starves people. Plant agriculture feeds people, uses less oil, less water, creates less pollution. We are using fresh water and food grains to feed animals. The statistics are dire: producing one kilogram of animal protein requires one hundred times more water than one kilogram of plant-based protein. The nine billion livestock we consume every year weigh five times as much as ourselves. The United States population has doubled in my lifetime, and will double again in the next seventy years, reducing the non-renewable fuels that sustain us now, along with water and topsoil; this is an unsustainable system. For more information on this, go to: http://www.ajcn.org/content/78/3/660S.full.pdf Sustainability of meat-based and plant-based diets and the environment1–3 David Pimentel and Marcia Pimentel.

Barbarity inflicted upon animals can spill into a hatred for our own species. Written on a stockyard gate confining a herd of goats is the graffiti, "god help us we cannot change." We need to rework concepts of good and evil, for after witnessing so much animal cruelty, all that comes to the stunned mind is that the perpetrators are evil. Theodor Adorno says, "Auschwitz begins whenever someone looks at a slaughterhouse and thinks: they are only animals." My concern, since being a child and growing up next to a hog farm and a block away from a slaughterhouse, is what goes on behind the scenes, what is being concealed, and how are we complicit by our silence. When will Toto trot up to that curtain and see not a wizard of great powers, but a sinister economic machine that profits from death? How much is concealed from us to enable us to consume and be entertained by animals, programming us to be passive and compliant, accepting this just the way it is? Our strength as a species is that we collaborate to survive. Our weakness as a species is that we are now collaborating with economic forces that intend we do not survive. The large cities of the world are fed into by arteries of highways, with trucks moving through empty streets at night carrying millions of live animals to be rendered into meat while we sleep. What kind of species are we that breeds other animals only to murder them? It is we who are being genetically altered both by our diet and our forced isolation from reality, and faster than even Darwin could conceive.

I watched a goat waiting to be slaughtered, put my fingers through the wire to rub her head. The temperature was already over one hundred degrees Fahrenheit. Only her number, a piece of hard, yellow plastic punched into her ear, made her individual, different from the hundreds of other goats in that pen. But to me, she was unique, with her own life, family, experiences. She waited patiently to be slaughtered. It's far from the slaughterhouse to your house. Another image in my memory is of a cow with a broken back or leg; they put her in the restraining pen, but the lunch siren sounded and all the workers left. I was alone with her in the slaughterhouse with all the blood and hanging bodies. She could not rise up, but kept kicking the sides of the steel pen like a Morse code that tapped out "help me," as she continually collapsed. The milk from her udders mingled with the blood of the other cows slaughtered before her and went down the drain. After thirty or so minutes, the workers returned and shot her through the brain with a captive bolt gun, and then in moments she was made into parts, starting with the stripping off of her face, which hung like a scarf around her neck. All the other cows in her family were lined up in steel corridors, trembling, waiting to be killed. These gentle and curious animals are subject to every type of abuse imaginable. Even in the hands of benign masters their unnatural, short lives end in a slaughterhouse. Dairy cows are bred to be gentle, bred to be handled.

Goat outside slaughterhouse
P.A.

Children and adults can see with their own eyes, if they get a chance, that animals are intelligent, capable of loyalty, understand their environment, and have an entire range of emotions and culture. We can see what happens to them when tails are docked or horns cut off. Fishes slowly suffocate in nets, piglets' testicles are gouged out, calves' ears are notched, beaks and claws are severed from fowl. We can see what happens to an animal not designed to live past his or her slaughter weight. Their legs cannot hold them up and their beaks no longer exist to peck the ground. Their wings are cut, or their hooves or claws, rendering them so crippled by living on concrete and wire that they cannot hobble. People who still have a semblance of mind left are changed forever when they see their food has a face and eyes that avoid our gaze. How would the food on our plate be different if we could see the terrible routine cruelties that are standard industry practice: animals abandoned without food and water, legs frozen solid in their own waste, dying in transport trucks on the way to be slaughtered—their short lives spent being roughly handled, electrocuted with cattle prods, drugged up with hormones and antibiotics, branded, beaten with tire irons, chained, noses pierced, fins cut off, gasping and torn apart in nets, bombed underwater, driven mad by life imprisonment, their babies stolen, being made repeatedly into breeding machines, entirely and utterly under the power and control of human beings. And all this with no language to communicate to this alien species, their oppressors, other than cries which go unheard. The latest in the list of abuses was last month in Pennsylvania, an intensive hog farm: the pigs were left in their cages to starve to death. Some had crawled outside, only to die. One thousand of them, and no one noticed, no one heard or saw. Our culture trains us to consume "happy meat" from the "happy farm." The meat industry regularly feeds us images of cows in buttercup pastures, lamb frolicking in clover, chickens in straw nests, always blue sky and sunshine. To see anything else, to see the reality of the filthy feed lots and sheds packed with millions of animals living in the near dark, to slip through the blood and entrails in a slaughterhouse full of knives, to hear the sound of their screams and the clanking of chains, the cursing of the workers, and continue to consume animals, would make us complicit. We want to remain innocent and oblivious, shame-free. But it's not possible; denial works for only so long. In the Romani language, the Holocaust is known as Porrajmos. It means "the devouring."

Mental depression works like tear gas. There is the soft hiss of it in every shopping mall, every supermarket, on the perimeter of the packaged goods, in those aisles where it gets cold. There are the cut-up bodies, their flesh shining pinkly through the cellophane packaging. Despite the cold, there is a stench of a corpse that air-conditioning cannot mask. No one ever looks over the top shelf, over the roof, over the car park, down the road, to the slaughterhouse and the factory farm. We are trained like geishas to look down, to take shuffling steps to the check-out counter, to look into our purses for the required remittance.

Alongside this final aisle of reckoning are magazines of glamour, airbrushed celebrities with gleaming white fangs—their lives are important, their tragedies and relationships—but still we reach down into the shopping cart and pick up the frankenfood with forty chemical ingredients and a picture on it to tell us what it is; it is something whose real life and death we shall never know about. A great cloud of depression, alleviated only by the temporary high of buying something, follows us into the car park like a ghost.

Susie works at Farm Sanctuary, an American farm animal protection organization. She told us of a case where she and the team went to rescue sows who had been kept in gestation crates all of their lives. The hog farms were all flooded, but one sow had swum to a levee and stayed alive there for three days. She had somehow rescued all of her piglets, nudging them up on the levee with her snout, away from the torrential waters, but by that time they were all dead bodies. The pork industry says that these crated sows have no emotional bond with their piglets, that it has long since been bred out of them. The government had ordered all the surviving pigs, who had somehow escaped their cages, to be shot. These pigs had never seen daylight, so they had third-degree burns on their skin from being outside.

The crime is our economic system, and the time is now for this tragedy to unfold: a catastrophe of species extinction, disease, and pollution. Western industrialized nations slipped, or rather were pushed, into the clutches of the system with eyes wide shut hundreds of years ago, when people were forced off the land and into economic growth and overproduction at any cost. The losses shared, the gains privatized. Can the current system be changed into an economic system that is in balance with the biosphere? For corporations, hedge funds, banks, their salespeople, and politicians, all disaster is a win-win. Climate change makes them trillions, wars make trillions, sickness makes trillions, "humane meat" makes profit, and factory-farmed meat makes profit. It's all short-term profit looking for the next tragedy to exploit. If shame were a currency, the rich would be drowning in their own blood money.

If we do not change, then we go under. It's always been a mystery to me why the wealthy do not appear to care for the future of their own children: that they would trash the earth, and not care for their progeny. We are on the Titanic now, only some of us sit in deck chairs. In the olden times, people went outside, went to demonstrations, talked to people face-to-face (not by Bluetooth), had direct confrontations, were loud, got messy. Now people sit in front of a glowing screen. Progressive politics is like watching a glacier melt (pre-climate change), but corporate crony capitalism, and the politicians who sell it to us, is the witnessing of wars and destruction at the speed of light. There is no choice but to struggle onward, because to not speak out is to be part of the conspiracy of silence. But to expect results is infantile, we must try for everything and expect nothing in our lifetimes.

We despair for the fate of animals, the senseless cruelties inflicted upon them by our species, their and our seeming helplessness in the face of mass slaughter—all this is true. We see it, we peer into the darkness when most others look away. Alongside is another truth about clinging to despair, and repeatedly feeling for it, like the tongue returning to a rotting tooth: the fall into misanthropy, the hatred of humans—that mental impulse is about the same old human power and control, not empathy. Yet there is another mysterious truth, but it's a secret and it's magical; all animals and plants know this secret: the ones with roots, that cannot run away, those with four legs, those with fins, those with fur, those with shells and scales, those with carapaces, and those with feathers; the ones that crawl under the earth, and the ones that fly at night, the luminous ones that have the power to glow, they whisper it every day—that there is a palpable goodness all around, even within us, even in the most terrible times, that all things are linked with. Somehow we have to educate ourselves not to swallow the bitterness and rage and even knowledge of watching life on this planet be destroyed, to recognize that we are less than grains of sand in the scheme of things, a billion flea creatures so tiny that we cannot see a billion other flea creatures living on us, residing some-where on one of a billion stars that, though we "see" them in the night sky, themselves ceased to exist many lifetimes ago, in a void whose length and breadth our human minds cannot even approach. Our brains never evolved to see clearly. We have only partial glimpses of truth, as though illuminated by lightning, only for a fraction of a second. If we could really see what we have done to the earth, we would go mad with sorrow. If only we could see the gift of living on this planet, we would go mad with joy. If the universe has a heartbeat, it would beat with love and pity for all of us. And who knows? This planet, our home, could already be stardust, seen from other planets as a shining star that no longer exists.

We are so frustrated at the lack of progress that we want to cannibalize each other, like a fox in a trap gnawing her leg off. Progress is being made, but it's difficult to see the effects when you live in the eye of the hurricane.

Millions of people who would not consider themselves "leaders" do the day-to-day care and rescue of animals all over the world. Those who show up at the pound every day, to give an abandoned dog or cat one last treat or kind word before they are murdered, who go over walls into slaughterhouses to video the crimes there, risking their own lives and prison, who stop on a busy highway to rescue a turtle with a crushed shell, who give a drink of water to a parched animal in a truck going to slaughter, who face mock-ery and derision by giving up the consumption of animal products in a meat-obsessed culture, and those who petition, who march, write letters, donate what little money they have, who legally represent animals, and who give them sanctuary, who patiently work through a mountain of ignorance, without anger and rage . . . and will never give up. No country or culture or language is any barrier to animal activists, who are everywhere.

Outside BARNES Slaughter House, Arizona 8am

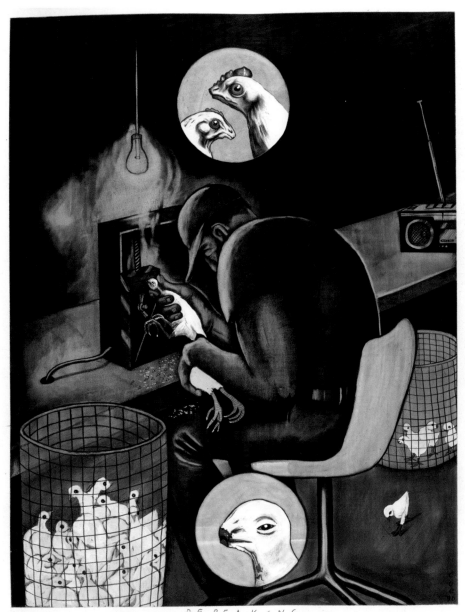

DE BEAKING
15 birds a minute - burned or severed tongues result in worthless hens

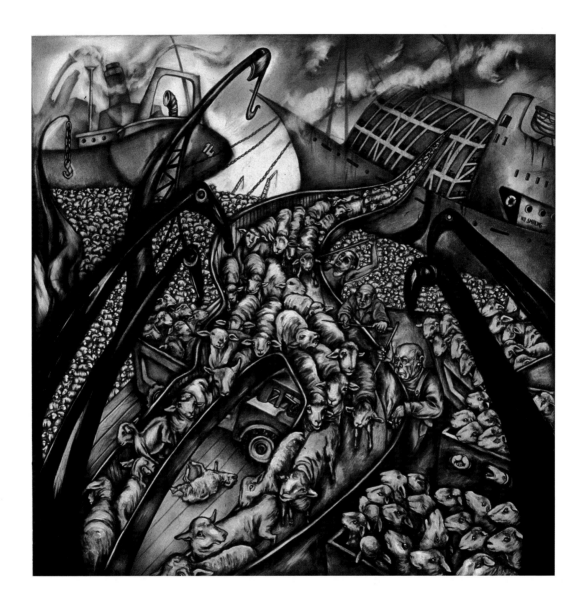

Entrance to Slaughterhouse

BROWN COW

Just today, I looked down from my studio, which is on the side of a mountain, and into the farm below. We are located in the epicenter of logging, hunting, fishing, gas well drilling, mining, and dairy farming, more commonly known as rural America. This farm has black and brown beef cattle. It is considered a "free range" beef farm. Many folks around here are involved with animal agriculture. Even though they have other jobs, they may use their land to finish cattle, or run a few beef. Last week, the owner slaughtered some of the animals to sell at the Oktoberfest celebration. A notice in the local newspaper explained a customer could select from the herd some living meat.

The flesh is advertised as "home grown."

The stench of the barbecuing, that sickly, greasy smoke smell, evokes a gag reflex, suffocates the beauty of autumn, the yellow and red falling leaves, the honk of migrating geese, the large pumpkins and late tomatoes.

Each day I walk down and look, because there is one cow that always returns my gaze, makes eye contact. She stands out from the rest, because she is a very unusual and beautiful light dusky brown color, a "Brown Swiss" with no white splashes. The orange tag in her ear stands out.

When summer was in full heat, the farmer, whose family also owns a dairy farm a few miles away where all the cows have docked tails, brought two tiny calves (Holsteins), barely as big as dogs, and dropped them in the meadow with the herd. The corn field had just been harvested, and the herd was competing with crows eating up the chaff. The two little calves were odd, being black and white, and they were so young that they could barely stand.

One day I saw that the two orphans were suckling from the dusky brown cow, and that they would follow her everywhere. She always guarded, wary, looking around on the alert. In the past, when it was a dairy farm, the cows would come up to my home to graze, as far as they could run away from the tin sheds of the farm. They would run, nearly up into the woods, sometimes they even escaped through a broken fence into the forest and would hide for days until the men with ATVs chased them down.

All summer I watched her with the calves, her willingness to be a foster mother, and I was filled with a deep sadness that such lives are manipulated for profit, without a second thought, by "animal husbands," who gain from this cow's endless supply of milk and her unlimited supply of compassion.

Even in the prison of the modern farm, she extended herself to help the little calves. She followed her instinct to nurture two babies who would have died without her.

Yesterday I went to see her. They had put electric wire between her and the calves. They had gotten as close as they could to each other without being shocked. The time had come for them to be forcefully separated. Neither the calves nor the brown cow were eating as the rest of the herd were—they just yearned to be together again. They knelt on the ground, facing each other, noses nearly touching. Three strands of hot wire separated them physically, but they were not yet separate, her breath was still their breath.

They Will Never See Each Other Again   Sue Coe 2010

Every animal knows and fears the gaze of human eyes, even from a mile away, and is aware. I want to tell her that I will never eat her, drink her milk, kill her or her babies. Dairy cows are bred to be handled by human beings, but their fear of humans has not been bred out of them.

In the winter, I drive past the other farm, the dairy farm. There is a big billboard promoting milk that creates a shadow over the farm. It can dip to 15 below in this area, and yet the replacement heifers are chained in white plastic kennels, chains around their tiny necks, separated from each other in a chessboard pattern. Never a soft kiss from the muzzle, or a touch of kindness; never the warmth of any living being. These calves are never touched, except when they are torn from their mothers, when holes are punched in their ears for tags, pliers tear off their horns, and their tails are docked. They shiver and they lie in the snow, preferring the cold outside to the plastic kennel. They move as far as the chain allows, a few feet. Their breath is icy.

I have asked farmers why this is done, and they say that the survivability of the calf in the natural state, with the mother, leads to higher mortality.

Sometimes lifespan and having a life are not the same.

The younger farmers are infected with words that justify the abuse of animals, contagion by degrees in animal agriculture. They know everything of the language of animal husbandry, which has become a science for corporate power. The irony is that they are the small farmers, the first to be cast aside for the giant CAFOs. What the small farmer and the CAFOs share is that the animal is reduced to parts, is a commodity, a product. It's reductionist thinking. The wholeness of the being is lost. Some small farmers may call their animals names, but they end up sold, to be rendered in the same slaughterhouses as the animals with no names. Most farmers are "good" people, just trying to follow in the family business, the only life they have known for generations.

The cows herd together on the other side of the electric wire, distraught, bending their necks as far as possible without getting stunned, in the hope of a scent or glimpse of their newborns. I have heard them cry out for their calves all day and night.

I rarely see any human being at these farms—no one to observe the animals or check if their water is frozen. Someone must do it. Sometimes the replacement heifers get tangled in their chains, and I wait to see if they can release themselves before going on my way. I see another farmer sometimes drive out in his air-conditioned or heated backhoe, when the ground is not frozen, to bury a calf. The corpse goes into the cornfield in a shallow grave. Before I lived here, he would dump the dead bodies of cows and calves up here out of sight, near the woods, and they would be consumed by vultures. It would take a week for a cow to completely disappear.

Hunting season will begin soon, and the sounds of gunfire will echo in the mountains. The herd will stay in the pasture until the deep snow forces them down nearer to the filth of their rickety sheds, where they will stand in a few feet of frozen mud and shit for five months, waiting for the backhoe to arrive with their feed. Until that time, the cows sleep together under the stars, in a tight group, or rest in the shade of the few trees, and when the deer and their fawns run out of the woods, frightened by the gunfire, they will mingle with the cows, trying to hide. When it is dark and the moon is bright, the coyotes will come out to sing and play. I have seen the young cows play games of chase with coyotes and rabbits for hours.

Today I went down the meadow trying not to look for the brown cow. Now she does not look at me. The calves have gone. How many of her calves have been stolen from her? When her time comes, as dictated by the meat industry not her own life span, she will be taken in a truck to a slaughterhouse to stand in line with her own kind. I don't want to look for her either, I don't want to see her not there. At her end, she will be in a steel restraining pen, and, shaking, she will look into the eyes of the man who will put a bolt into her brain—then, still alive, she will be hoisted into the air while her throat is cut. As her blood is gushing out, her last sight will be the other skinned and decapitated cows moving to the next disassembling of their lives, some of whom could be her own calves or her own mother.

The Government Inspector

Cows and Calves waiting to be auctioned. they will never see each other again   Sue Coe 2010

PECKED TO DEATH

I was drawing young turkeys—they were confined within a large cage. Turkeys are truly amazing, their colors and friendliness, their curiosity. If you visit Farm Sanctuary, rescued turkeys will happily come over and sit on your lap to get stroked.

One young bird had got a tiny speck of dark blood on her white wing, the result of a peck, or getting caught on the wire, but this speck triggered the pecking instinct of the other birds, who, if they had been born into freedom as wild turkeys, would be pecking at the ground, at bark, at grasses, looking for any seed or insect. The birds in confinement were compelled to make that speck larger—the victim bird would give a high-pitched cry—a cry for a mother. The parent bird would have heard this cry through the woods and come to the rescue.

But not here.

The bird would cry out, run to the side of the cage and stand against the bars; there would be a brief respite. The other birds knew nothing of cruelty—they just knew they had to peck and they had not yet been de-beaked, and they knew where the speck was and could not leave it alone, eventually returning to it like a red magnet, over and over again. The bird would cry again, and move again, but this was one bird, in a cage with five others. When one bird stopped pecking, another would take over. The victim could never rest. I watched as the bird fell asleep on her feet, sank to the ground, desperate for sleep. The thin, blue eyelids would cover her eyes, and another bird would start pecking, startling her into waking. At some point in my observation, the bird would sleep through the pain for a few seconds, and then wake up. Eventually the speck would be a large ragged wound, and the wound would get infected and the bird would die.

I had my sketchbook and was drawing and drawing—spent an hour drawing—and during that time, many people would glance in the cage and move on; they looked but never stayed long enough to see.

What drawing reveals is the intimacy of shared time. My drawing of chicks in a cage became witnessing the start of a tragic end. I did look at how to unlock the cage (could not) and hatched a dream of rescuing the bird. This scene takes place a billion times, inside cages or inside sheds packed with chickens or turkeys. I know that observing the real life and dying of this bird is not about the many words and pieces of information about the history of the meat industry, all the facts and data, the different perspectives that either justify the industry's existence as providing food or justify the end of animal production because of the cruelty and destruction of the environment. It's about identifying this one little helpless victim, who had no voice that was ever heard.

Play above the Honey Gatherers in the Sanderbans at the Tiger Camp Bengal India

HUNGER

In the region of Bengal, a few miles from Kolkata, is the Sunderbans, known as a sanctuary for tigers—the Bengal tiger. This highly endangered animal exists alongside villages protected with high wire fencing. The riverbanks of that area are being compromised by climate change, the rising sea water, and the eroding banks due to the fishing of the tiger shrimp, which is very valuable on the global market. It takes only a few drops of sea water, flooding back into the land, to destroy the sweet water with its acres of rice paddies. The constant task every day for the people is to find what is called sweet water, meaning not dirty, polluted, or salt water.

The tigers are hungry, and the Bengal tiger is the only tiger of its species that hunts and eats human beings.

For the vegetarian, Kolkata and Bengal offer quite possibly the best tasting food in the world. Any restaurant will have two menu sections, and the first and largest is vegetarian. Kolkata is surrounded by tiny farms—some are even within the city—that grow fresh vegetables every day and sell them by the road. A tomato or cucumber taste like they used to, before they tasted of fish: a burst of pure flavor. A family's one skinny cow, or goat, or duck, is a precious family member, as recognizable to the village as any human would be, and is moved many times a day to eat the few tufts of greenery.

Unlike the poor in the United States, many of whom are obese, while the wealthy are as gym-slender as could be, only rich Indians are fat, for they have the money to eat at the western restaurants. Most Indian people are thin and work very hard, and they work hard to get their food. The global meat industry has its greedy eye on India, with the plan of manufacturing animals for a higher caloric intake, their concern for the starving masses the selling point. But the reality is expansion and profit and no environmental impediments.

There is no doubt that Indian people in general are not getting sufficient calories, but it is not because they do not consume meat, it is because of the colonialist history of forcing the people to grow white rice instead of higher protein grains such as millet. Beguiled with stories of greater yields and profit and aggressive marketing campaigns, Indian farmers got into debt to buy terminator seeds (seeds that cannot produce viable seeds by themselves) such as those manufactured by Monsanto, and they stopped farming with traditional seeds. These so-called "magic seeds" became murderous. The price difference is staggering—one thousand times more to purchase genetically modified seeds. When crops fail and famine or floods arrive, farmers cannot pay off their spiraling debt. A shocking number of farmers, estimated at 125,000, both male and female, have killed themselves—many by drinking the pesticides that are needed for the genetically engineered seeds—and dying in agony. When crops failed in the past, the farmer always kept seeds to replant.

Unlike beguiled mortgage holders in the United States who at least have a chance of reading a contract, if not understanding it, the small farmer in India cannot read. Farmers are losing their land and becoming the landless poor, begging on the streets of Mumbai and Kolkata. But the people are fighting back: one state is suing Monsanto.

Food is life and death, and nowhere quite exemplifies this struggle between food and culture like the Sunderbans.

The road from Kolkata to the Sunderbans is Blakian: dark, satanic mills, chemical plants with pollution coming from stacks so thick and dense, the dark dust of it covers the red dust of India. In between the chemical factories are tiny farms and everyone sells the extra that they have grown that day. On a clean cloth on the side of the road, a seller would have lined up two cucumbers or a tomato or a tiny teaspoonful of spice, and by selling that, they would be able to live another day. Also alongside the road would be thousands of washed saris drying in the breeze, their gemlike colors contrasting with the dusty air.

The "Goddess of the Forest" is called Bonobibi, and her image can be found on any jungle or swamp clearing; she is worshipped in almost every village of Bengal. Dakhsin Rai is the "Tiger God," and he is worshipped under the banyan tree. The tiger gods came from the time of the Muslim invasion. There are gods to protect snakes, and cows and to prevent cholera; they all have to be appeased. I was told there is peaceful harmony between Christians and Muslims and Hindus, a forced, peaceful coexistence. The Gunins and the Ojhas are like village doctors who are attributed with supernatural powers to heal snakebites and protect from tigers. One of those was our guide. The Sunderbans are a deeply mysterious place, as complex as its natural terrain. Tigers are both feared and worshipped. Along the banks of the river, on the way to the Bay of Bengal, is the Village of Widows—women who have lost their husbands to the tiger. As the tiger is both protected and revered it never occurs to anyone, even those who have lost limbs to tigers, to kill them. We heard stories of daring rescues from Bengal tigers, who have the skill to swim out into the river, overturn the fragile boats, and take humans. This area has been developed since 300 BC, and one of the main jobs, then and now, is honey gathering. To do this, the men leave the safety of the village and go forth into the swamps, where the tigers live. They believe the tiger has more rage against humans because of the seawater flooding into the delta, and that this incites them to kill. No other tiger in India kills humans unless wounded. The honey gatherers also believe that a tiger will attack only from behind, bite at the back of the neck, and drag the prey away, so they wear plastic masks of the gods and goddesses on the back of their heads, where they are most vulnerable, when climbing up the trees to get the honey. Like many other species, such as the butterfly or the hawk, eyes can appear to be on the back of the head to ward off predators.

The villagers told us that they had wrestled with the tigers when they had already a death grip on a friend or relative, but that this person nearly always died. We wanted to see a tiger at the beginning of this journey, but then decided we preferred not to, as we were in a small boat. We witnessed how people respect non-human life while risking their own lives to get food. They believe that if they die by tiger, it is because sufficient offerings have not been made the gods.

At night we sat behind security fences and watched plays enacted of this struggle for honey, of growing crops and feeding the people, and of the tigers. Imagine working so hard all day, and then at night, putting on stage makeup with sparkly costumes to act out stories that are thousands of years old. My sister and I thought they were professional actors, and the "actors" thought that was so funny. For them art and life are the same thing. By the light of the moon and a fire, we ate delicious food that was grains and vegetables, and watched songs and dancing and stories. The tigers would roar at night and the people were safe in their villages. It was magical and humbling.

India, China, and Brazil, and the global south, are ripe pickings for the expansion of CAFOs, as the market for cheap soy and corn is being diverted to ethanol in the United States, along with a growing awareness of the massively destructive footprint of industrial meat production.

China is no stranger to starvation—the same people that used to eat grass now eat tiger and bear paw, monkey and snake and hawks, crocodile, and if they could dine on hummingbird tongues they would.

Tigers are factory farmed in China, placed in battery cages to pace and go insane, and then made into product. The Chinese authorities say these farms are critical to conservation efforts and discourage poaching, much like zoos who breed endangered species say in the United States. The effect is the opposite: a greater demand for tiger bones, meat, body parts, and tiger wine, where the corpse of the tiger rots in containers until a "wine" is produced. Chinese tigers are now down to a pathetic 20 to 50 in the wild—functionally extinct. This may be the last Year of the Tiger in China. Ninety-five percent of Chinese polled supported the idea of banning tiger products, yet fifty-five percent of them stated that they had used tiger products in the past, and a large percent of those said they preferred wild tiger products over factory farmed.

They stayed alive in a closed slaughterhouse for one week with no water or food
they waited for us to rescue them.

Sue Coe 2010

LIVING GHOSTS

It was at the height of the summer when a cow escaped from a slaughterhouse. She jumped a gate, and ran and ran, and was captured on the city streets by the police . . . who called her a bull because she still had horns.

Her escape had made her visible: people now saw one cow desperate for life and felt pity. The incident was too publicly visible for her to be returned to the slaughterhouse and slaughtered along with the millions of others that day, so she was taken to Farm Sanctuary.

The slaughterhouse was closed by the "health department" for allowing the cow to escape and because of the complaints of neighbors who were disturbed by the "screaming of animals." Numerous violations were found, and a temporary halt in slaughtering was ordered along with an order to vacate.

Farm Sanctuary inquired if there were any other animals locked inside? Were they being fed and watered? Where were they?

A phone call was made to the owner, and he said there were still animals in the slaughterhouse, but what could he do? It was closed.

He was asked if he was providing food or water. No, he said, he was not allowed to go in there.

Farm Sanctuary asked if the animals could be rescued and cared for. The owner said he would pray to Allah, and if Allah said we could take them, then he would allow it. The next day, after numerous phone calls, days after the place was closed, he told us that Allah would want us to take the animals, so we set off in a large trailer with a map to find the location. The journey was long and difficult—we had no idea what we would find. Would any animals still be alive?

We stayed at a motel halfway through the journey and spent a sleepless night worrying about the animals. Would we be too late?

We found the address, and like most places of this kind, the building was just a regular, blank factory-looking building, concealed in the sort of neighborhood that is called "transitional"—middle-class people moving into what used to be a working-class area, with developers just waiting to make a profit. The first thing I noticed was a jogger running past. She had an iPod plugged into her head, long legs and short shorts. As we were waiting for someone to come with the keys and open the doors of the place, she shouted that the place stank and should be closed down. She had that petulant anger of outrage, and the confidence of her class, to shout at strangers—and that anger was directed at us, as though we worked there. We waited, and various people walked past: a woman with an expensive stroller. The boss came with a bunch of keys and some other guys, who stood around on the sidewalk smoking and joking. They were the slaughterhouse staff, but nervous under the façade of bravado, their nervousness camouflaged in macho jokes as they slouched against the wall. They had known the animals were in there and had just abandoned them to a slow death.

The large doors were unlocked. It was a hot summer morning; the light was so blinding. Inside was completely dark and silent. The air was thick.

We walked inside, trying get our eyes to adjust, and finally were able to make out hundreds of cages, some four tiers high—ducks and geese, turkeys and chickens—and into each cage were stuffed eight or so animals. Many were dead, with the living at the top of the dead piles; all those who had waited days for us to come and rescue them. Those that were alive, their feathers had all fallen out, sometimes to just tufts. The bare wire cages were caked with excrement and partially decayed corpses. All those days that we ate and drank and slept, they had starved and died. It seems impossible that they could live this long without water, and all the time, only a few feet away, people were carrying on with their lives, rushing along the city streets, oblivious.

We worked quickly to load up the animals into the truck. They desperately tried to escape us, thinking they had just survived a delay in the slaughter, they had panic and fear, were desperate to escape us. The temperature was in the 90s, and inside the slaughterhouse it was even higher.

The rescue volunteers were adept and purposeful and worked very fast to load up the birds. I picked up a goose that had fallen from a cage—she was as thin as paper, and hot as I clutched her to my chest—and I could feel her beating heart against my own, beating so fast. I felt I was in a dream; the other rescuers were so professional and had seen all of this before. All the animals left alive were skeletal. We stared into the last cages to see any eyes, any movement.

To say the journey to safety was very difficult is an understatement. Most of the animals were desperately thirsty. We stopped off at a gas station along the route and I got some water for a few of the animals in a paper cup. We could not water them because it would take too long, and they were so stressed that they needed to get out of the hot truck as fast as possible. I offered the paper cup to the few birds that could get to it, and they drank from it as though it was life, which it was.

The animals that lived stayed together for the rest of their lives, not joining other animals of the same species at the sanctuary, but staying in a tight group with their slaughterhouse brethren, the survivors— the goose protected the tiny chicken, putting her under a wing all night, for they had been in the same cage together, alive and alone, at the top of a rotting pyramid of corpses. Their feathers grew back, glossy and shiny. What did they remember? Did they have nightmares? The goose's protection of the chicken continued long past their rescue from the slaughterhouse. I visited the goose in her new home. She loved her life, and walked on grass for the first time, sat on hay bales, balanced on fences like a tightrope walker, and roosted with a tiny chicken all night, her large wing sheltering this shy bird.

Sue Coe 10

THE SHEEP SHEARER

A sheep shearer was doing a demonstration shearing in the middle of a shopping mall and I went along to draw, as it is one of the few trades that has not changed in hundreds of years, and for an artist, it's a perfect opportunity to draw the human figure in constant motion.

The shearer had brought ten of his own sheep who had grown long wool. It smelled of hay and meadows and sunshine and retained woolly memory of running through the woods, snaring thorns and seed pods. One of the sheep had a lamb with her. Sheep are flock creatures; they feel safe and secure only when they're all together, and these sheep stayed in a little huddle in front of the stores in the mall: the Gap, Starbucks. Their hooves tapped on the shiny mall floor. They stayed in a tight circle.

The shearer brought out a sheep. His small daughter, aged ten, helped him—she had dressed for the special occasion in her best party dress, a flimsy diaphanous pink princess dress. She wanted to please her father, and watched for his commands.

He flipped the sheep onto her back. This motion for shearers becomes harder over time—their backs eventually fail—so shearing is for younger men. They travel all over the country and sometimes all over the world to do this work. It is highly paid, but seasonal. For some ancient reason known only to sheep, once they are upside down on their backs, they remain in a paralyzed state, without struggling—it may have been a response to predators—and can be manipulated by the sheep shearer. The shearer makes the same movements over and over with the electric clippers. I cannot imagine shearing hundreds of sheep a day with manual iron shears; they are so heavy, hands would have been covered in blisters. It takes very precise movements to take a sheep's coat, for their coat to become our coat.

When the sheep with the lamb was brought out from the group, she panicked and struggled—her lamb was showing great distress—so the young girl held onto the lamb, and brought him into the ring with his mother so they could still see each other. It never occurred to me that what had been the lamb's secret, the teats of his mother, would suddenly be exposed to an entire crowd of mall shoppers. Without their wool covering, they were revealed, pink and damp, nicked with bleeding cuts, their shared secret no longer. The lamb struggled desperately to be with his mother, and when she was finally released, they ran to each other and were immediately calmed. The fear of the clippers, the people, the noise of the generator disappeared as they were together again.

I asked the shearer about the lamb. How old was he? He had tiny horn buds and was all black. The shearer said in another week the lamb would go for slaughter, as he was a male, "and you only need one of those." He laughed. I wondered if he had sons, and how many lambs had this mother lost? How many times had she been bred and given birth, and then lost her lambs? Standing together in that moment, mother and child, they had no idea that next week they would never see each other again. They were together—that is all they knew.

It was early spring, and snow was still on the ground, the sheep were shivering, and on their skin ran the tracks left by the electric shearer.

GASSING HOGS

The largest hog slaughterhouses in the world now gas hogs. Pigs are unloaded from large trailer trucks that wait in line around the facility. The hogs are then moved from the truck into a waiting area. They do not want to leave the truck, and electric cattle prods are employed to force them out. I have seen men repeatedly using the prod on pigs' eyes, shocking them in the eye to get them to move into the slaughterhouse. The sound of the pigs screaming is deafening to the human ear. Pigs panic and attempt to escape. They crawl over each other in desperation, they fall in between the truck and the pens, they are kicked and shoved and beaten to get into line. In the waiting area, they are continually misted with water to keep them hydrated. In the winter the pigs shiver. These days, the traditional captive bolt pistol method of stunning pigs is changing to gassing. The animal must be stunned, but not killed, so the beating heart can pump out the blood. "Pigs are stunned by submersion in a high CO_2 concentration (> 80%). However it is well known that pigs stunned with a gaseous mixture containing 86% CO_2 and air display obvious signs of respiratory distress (gasping, vocalizing) and adverse behavior. This is an indication of a deterioration in the animals' welfare status."[1] (Hoenderken, 1983; Troeger and Wolterdorf, 1991; EFSA, 2004) Expert opinion is divided concerning the amount of distress experienced during inhalation of high concentrations of CO_2 (Lambooij, 1999, Gerritzen 2000; Raj, 1995, Martoft, 2001). I have seen hogs stunned with the captive bolt pistol. The pigs are first roughly forced into the single-file chutes. As they move through in a single line, the gun is placed on their forehead and fired, destroying the brain matter: the brain stem is left intact to keep the heart beating, exsanguinating blood from the body. This method of stunning requires that the use of the pistol be precise and accurate, or the hog is not sufficiently stunned. Imprecise, inaccurate stunning increases as the line speed is increased. This means some pigs are conscious when exsanguinated and placed into the boiling tank to remove their bristles.

In the Smithfield plant in North Carolina, four gas chambers are used, and the pigs enter the chamber seven at a time. "Gassing causes less trauma for the animals and creates a better product; less muscle constriction means the meat is more tender, says Dennis Pittman, director of corporate communications."[2]

I have never witnessed hogs being gassed. To find out what this process entails, I found a video of several experiments with gas (CO2 mixtures) done by animal scientists in the Netherlands.[3] You can decide for yourself the level of trauma in these controlled conditions. For thirty seconds the pig gasps and cries, and tries to climb the glass walls of the chamber to escape. It is a long and terrible suffocation. Enter the world of Grandin Through the Looking Glass: designer of modern meat industry slaughterhouses, she of the oft-quoted observations as to what is "more humane" and what is "less." The cult of Temple Grandin pervades both the meat industry and animal welfare/rights groups.

I was asking local farmers about different methods of stunning cattle and hogs, and mentioned Grandin's approach to making slaughterhouses more "humane." A few of them were familiar with her work. I was surprised this was even a consideration for them, as they usually avoid all conversations about slaughter. Yes, they agreed that a more humane method of slaughter was preferable, but then, predictably, this was followed with the comment, "because the meat tastes better."

Temple Grandin has stated that because she is autistic—because of her deficiencies in reading human emotion—she can see the reality of an animal from that animal's viewpoint, and, indeed, she has shared some startling and unique observations of domesticated animals that enlighten us. Yet she also states that when she holds an animal's head in her hands as s/he is being slaughtered, she feels a deep, godlike connection to that animal. Which is it: godlike feelings or the clinical observations of the scientist? Perhaps neither.

What Grandin has become is the modern cult equivalent of the Judas Goat, an animal still used in ritual slaughterhouses in America. Such a goat, saved from the herd, leads the flock into the slaughter-house with a level of confidence and certitude that is lacking in badly paid meat packers who are forced into a level of violence that any "brutal" animal could not conceive. Grandin is rarely if ever questioned; everything she utters is accepted, for it is in no one's interest to question it. Of particular interest is her paper "Effect of genetics on handling and CO2 stunning of pigs." Apparently, breeds of hogs differ in terms of excitability and objection to being slaughtered. In her essay she notices the effect of the electric prods on pigs bred for rapid weight gain and leanness, and their predisposition toward hyper-reactivity when touched, extreme flocking instinct, and constant attempts to back out of the line into the kill floor. She uses this observation to justify gassing as an alternative to the single line system, and stunning with captive bolt pistol, quoting two studies to conclude, "There are two possible solutions to this increasing meat quality and welfare problem: Select pigs for a calm temperament, or develop CO2 stunning equipment where the use of a single file race could be eliminated." She further suggests, "Handling would be greatly improved if a group of five to ten pigs could be driven into a small pen that then descended into the gas." Grandin, who simultaneously balances the "problem" of welfare while developing and improving on the technology of the industrial disassembly line, is a useful creature to both those concerned for animal welfare and an industry that wants more killed for less labor. She uses empirical data to justify the myth that animals are food, bred only to be slaughtered.

The first time I witnessed a Judas Goat, he was watching me from a platform above the kill floor. I was alone, standing on slippery blood; all the animals had been disassembled, which gave me space to draw the machinery. I happened to look up, and a goat was looking down at me. I assumed this was someone's "pet" goat that had been rescued, and asked about him. One of the workers laughed and said this was a Judas and soon his time would come . . . when they got a better one. I am sure from the Judas viewpoint he was eyeing me with the idea that I had escaped, and he still had work to do.

The role of the Judas Goat in the Nazi death camps was played by the Sonderkommando, for a time, until he too was slaughtered. This prisoner directed the others, quelled panic, and provided a sense of order that kept those about to be killed in line. Like the Judas Goat, the Sonderkommando had to die and be replaced, to ensure the fate of all those entering the slaughterhouse remain a secret until it was too late to rebel. The two papers Grandin mentions on the gassing of hogs have slight differences in their observations of hogs in gas chambers, and reach different conclusions about the level of suffering (as determined by body movement and vocalizations) of the pigs being gassed: one infers that the excitation phase of being gassed occurs after the pig is no longer conscious; the other suggests the pig is still conscious and aware long into the process. Grandin neatly resolves this by stating that different breeds of hog respond differently and more study is needed. Her suggestion is that the industry should breed hogs that when gassed show no obvious signs of suffering. If they do not appear to suffer, then they are not suffering. Problem solved. Pork quality remains high. Reading this paper, one enters a worldview that is truly off-the-hook madness, bizarre and highly objectionable to those of us who do not believe that the mass slaughter of sentient beings for consumption is either necessary or acceptable. Unfortunately, animal activists are the ones commonly considered mad, residing as they do in a culture that improves on ways to make slaughter more palatable.

We all exist in a world with massive contradictions. The true horror lies not in exposing these contradictions, but rather in selling an illusion that the contradictions are resolvable or removable for the continuance of profit. Mass breeding and slaughter of animals is consistent with neither our own good health nor that of other beings, yet the production of animal products grows exponentially. It reduces us to unthinking, unfeeling machines. We have lost wholeness and interconnectivity. And Grandin, with bedfellows in both the meat industry and the more recent allies of animal activist organizations, is an economic tool of the meat industry. This brilliant woman, a born problem solver, is not as trapped in her trade as the sad, isolated goat. If she feels as isolated as an anthropologist from Mars, then for non-human animals we are the alien predators invading their world. Our society has become willingly unsighted, willingly promoting No Touch Torture on its victims. Poisoned with pollutants and violence, we avoid eye contact with what is about to become our meal, we have no desire to see inside the slaughterhouses where our "food" is prepared, we repress the intuition that killing is wrong, we make a mockery of people who have emotions about animals being killed, we make repeated and futile attempts to make capitalism more humane, we prefer to communicate via machines. Grandin has not looked away, she has not denied that animals suffer in the process of becoming our food; she has attempted to resolve what can never be resolved as long as we view animals as property. We all can try to make choices consistent with our values. It is not clear or even important where Grandin's values lie. It is important that our society find a way of existing that is consistent with the survival of the planet. Grandin is creating a more humane and efficient meat industry, and she is greasing the wheels of the killing machine, both. If she did not exist, the meat industry would have had to invent her.

NOTES

1. http://www.themeatsite.com/articles/678/stunning-of-slaughter-pigs-with-cosub2-subd

2. http://www.thepigsite.com/swinenews/18760/visit-to-worlds-largest-pig-plant

3. http://www.youtube.com/watch?v=N082tXCac08&NR=1

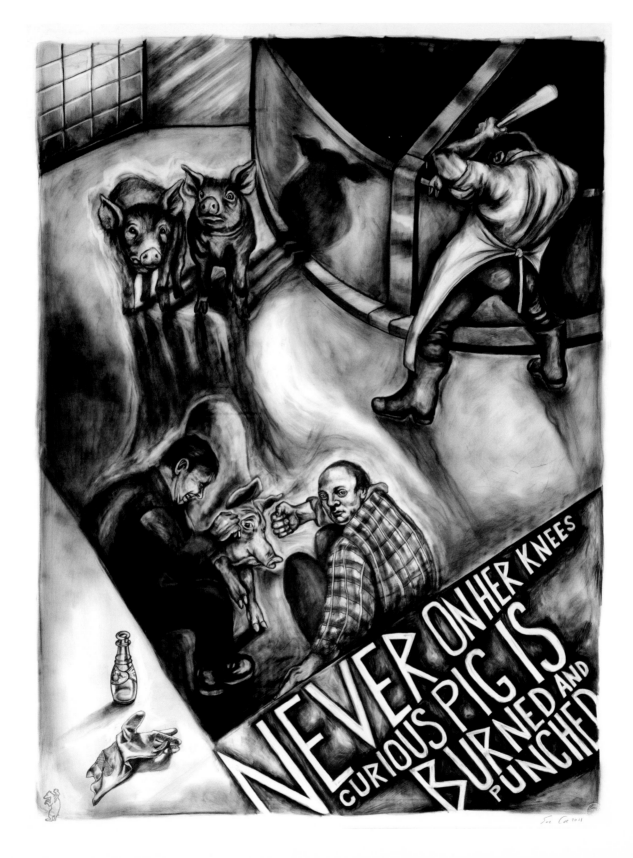

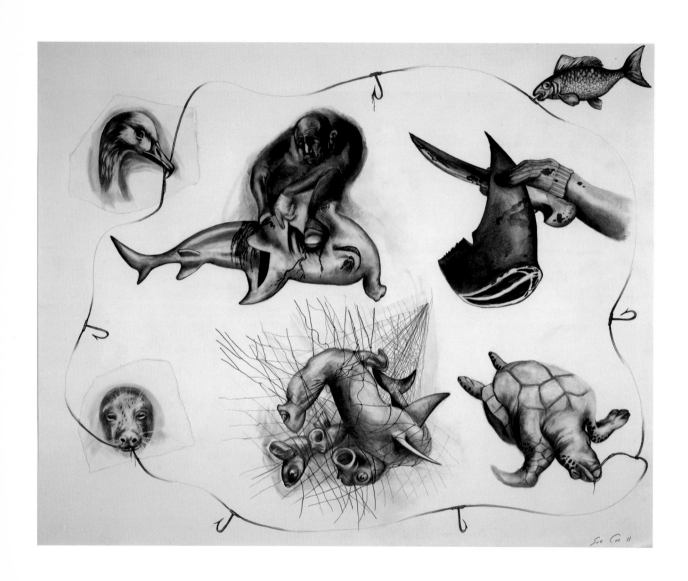

THERE ARE PLENTY
OF FISH IN THE SEA

"Fish die belly upward, and rise to the surface, it's their way of falling." —André Gide

"The factory-farmed pig is the largest aquatic predator. It takes seventy fish in the ocean to feed one factory-farmed salmon." —Paul Watson (captain of the Sea Shepherd)

The dying sea turtles and dolphins, the gummed-up pelicans, the suffocating sea birds, the grey coral, the acidic ocean: all are now predictable sights to us. Just the toxic runoff from factory farming and urban areas into the Gulf of Mexico created a dead zone the size of Massachusetts, the largest recorded in 2010—and this was before the BP disaster. Organisms that cannot flee the dead zone suffocate. This zone competes with other manmade disasters, the islands of plastic trash (one the size of Texas, one recorded to be as large as the United States) that now infest the oceans. One of the most poignant side-effects of this is the baby albatrosses choking on plastic syringes and magic markers fed them by their parents—the bright colors resemble small fish. Turtles consuming and choking on plastic bags, thinking they were jelly fish.

"The Gulf is our sushi bar, our toilet, and our gas station," said one observer after the BP spill.

I have often lain facedown, peering into our local pond, a world of watery mystery. My dogs and I strain to see beneath the surface, and when our eyes become adjusted there are hundreds of tiny fishes to be seen. They swim in unison at great speed, making a pattern—how do they collaborate? Do they sense the fragile movements of water and fins? Rarely will one explore alone; in seconds it darts back to its fishy nation. Smaller than a little fingernail, these fishes already have eyes, a heart, and a brain, an idea of symmetry. The pond contains millions of lives: do they look upward at the sky and clouds? Do they see that as part of their world, a ceiling? The pond knows nothing of the gas drilling, the fracking planned for the neighborhood next year, just as the tree does not fear the ax.

It's official now: scientists have declared that fish do indeed feel pain. Goldfish were boiled and injected with saline solution to prove the point. When placed back in their own home tank, they showed "fearful avoidance behavior." How do these studies impact the war on aquatic life? Probably they will have the same negligible impact as fish eaters being told they consume dangerous amounts of mercury—they care little. The drift nets, the factory farming, the tearing out of their gills, the hooking, spearing, bludgeoning, the slaughter of baby harp seals because they have the temerity to grow up and eat fish, all this will continue until there is nothing left. There are no humane regulations controlling the slaughter of fish. The larger ones such as salmon are clubbed over the head, smaller ones have their water drained, or are put on ice to suffocate. In the fish markets, the fish are cut up alive.

Bluefin tuna, sharks face annihilation: without these magnificent creatures oceanic ecosystems will collapse: the salty sea will be writhing with jelly fish. Tuna fishing has become a four-billion-dollar-a-year black market. One bluefin tuna went for $400,000 on the Japanese market this year. Their population numbers have decreased by eighty percent since 1970.

Just under half the fish consumed are raised in land- or ocean-based aqua farms. Drugs and genetic engineering are used to control reproduction. It is commonly estimated that up to forty percent of fish raised this way are blind. As the fish are so confined, they collide with each other, creating damage to fins and scales and allowing fecal matter and swarms of parasites to contaminate the fish's body. Along with the aqua farmer's antibiotics, this creates a toxic stew of chemicals that leeches into the wild.

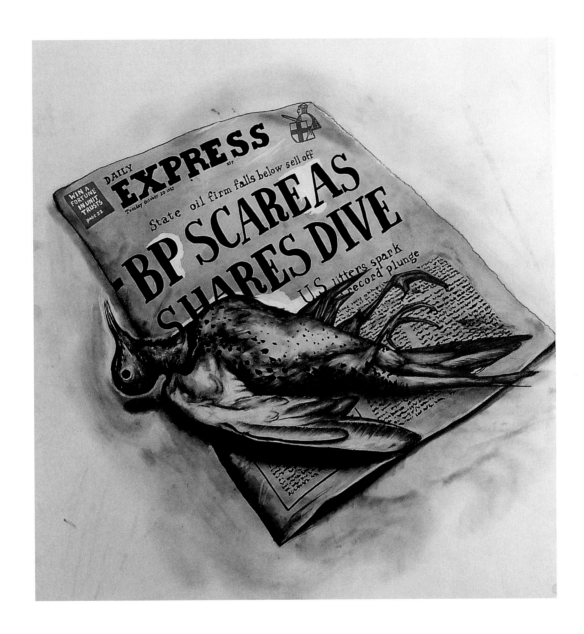

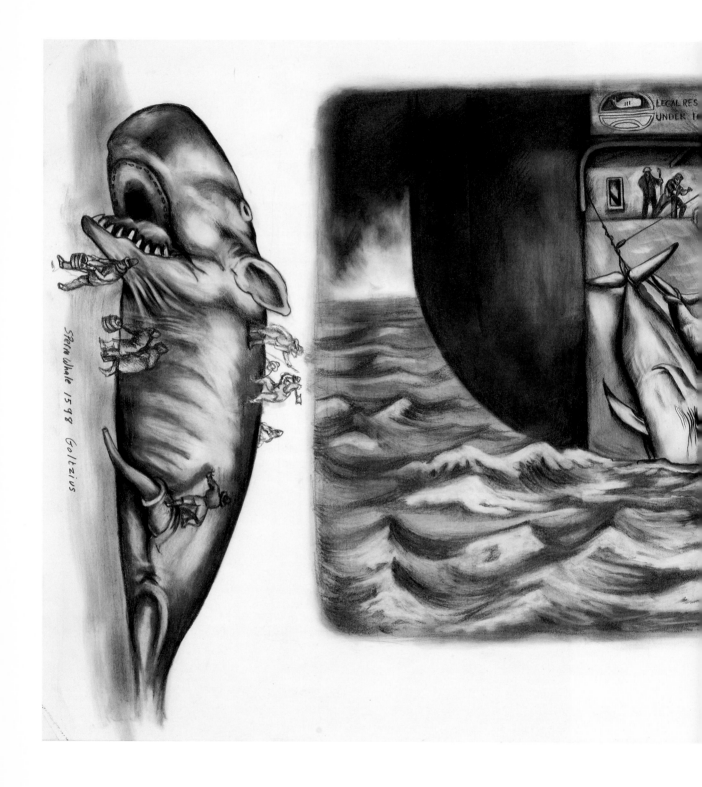

Stern Whale 1598 Goltzius

S O S

Sue Coe 11

Murder in the Gulf

Sold!   Sue Cox 10

B P - Burns Turtles

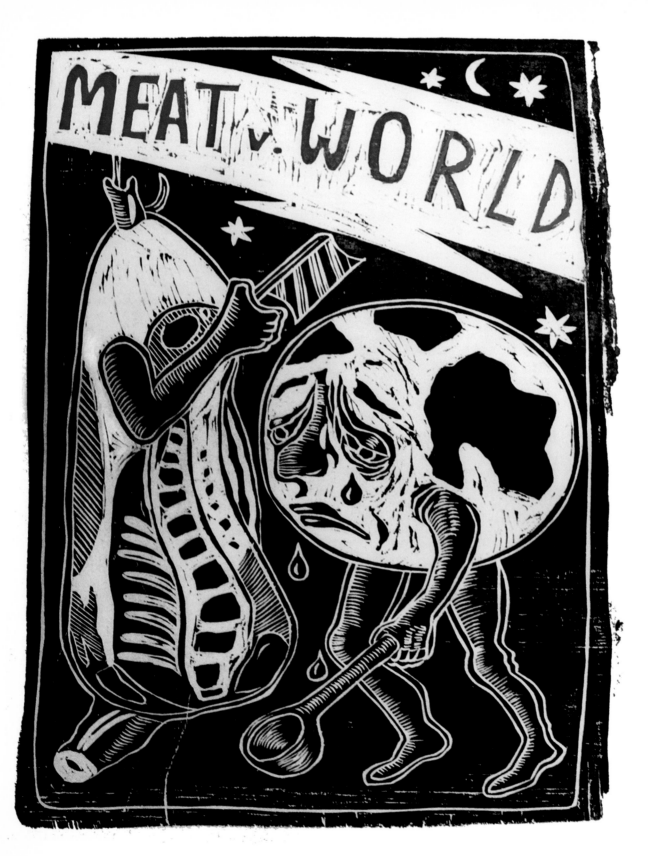

GERMS

"There is no need to sally forth, for it remains true that those things which make us human are, curiously enough, always close at hand. Resolve then, that on this very ground, with small flags waving and tinny blast on tiny trumpets, we shall meet the enemy, and not only may he be ours, he may be us." —Walt Kelly, The Pogo Papers[1]

We are at war with germs, and we are not winning. Things had been looking up after World War II. In contrast to nineteenth-century epidemics caused by Dickensian living conditions (poor sanitation, contamination of water supplies, and the pervasive adulteration of food and drink),[2] by the 1960s, the advance of infectious diseases was slowed by modern plumbing, stronger food and drug safety regulations, and better enforcement. Any stray microbe that might cause trouble was sure to be defeated by the new and potent drugs and vaccinations, to the point where some thought infectious diseases had been all but eradicated.

Since then however, outbreaks of bacterial food poisonings, viral plagues, formerly unknown pathogens and environmental depredations of soil, air, and water have stormed our inadequate defenses. We develop wonder drugs to attack the invading infection, but the infectious agent develops immunity to its antibiotic opponent. We produce more food, for less money, in less time, but the conditions under which the food is produced bring Mad Cow, *E. coli*, *Salmonella*, and staph infections to market. We risk becoming dead meat ourselves by consuming the tainted eggs, meat, milk, lettuce, peanut butter, pistachio nuts, and strawberries that evade the inevitable recalls.

Human and farmed animal populations constantly encroach upon the dwindling wild; once distant regions have become our neighbors but they still support reservoirs of virulent diseases, which now can spread worldwide in a matter of days. We are helpless to defend against unfamiliar microbes that we, in our ignorance, encourage and just as cluelessly propagate. This is a war, and we are the victims of friendly fire—our microscopic enemies have a powerful ally, one that we ourselves have created and continue to maintain—our tendency to push the envelope. We enlist antibiotics, chemical pesticides, and predicides (poisons designed to kill predators), ostensibly to protect our food sources and encourage bumper crops, but what happens when our food brings disease to the dinner table? What began with the earliest human civilizations, the domestication of animals, has now evolved into the global culture of industrialized food. In the process, the life-saving miracles of modern chemistry and medicine have turned against us. Penicillin is a case in point, but first a little history of medicine.

Medicine became modern when it shed mystical beliefs about the causes of disease and accepted a paradigm shift to the so-called germ theory of disease. That infectious diseases might be caused by tiny living beings, invisible to the naked eye, was at first considered self-evident nonsense, but the evidence mounted, and today no one questions the existence of bacteria or the success of the drug industry devoted to developing and testing natural or synthetic chemicals to combat those germs.

Anton van Leeuwenhoek was the first to see what we call bacteria, using a lens that he himself had ground and polished. His late seventeenth- and early eighteenth-century explorations of the microscopic world of life underpin modern cell biology and the practice of modern medicine. Fast-forward two centuries. By 1890, Robert Koch's germ theory of disease had gained a measure of general acceptance, putting to rest false notions of "spontaneous generation" or "miasmic air" as causative agents of disease. Thanks to Ignaz Semmelweiss, doctors now knew it was important to wash their hands after carrying out autopsies and before delivering babies; surgeries were cleaner than ever, thanks to Joseph Lister; Louis Pasteur's name became synonymous with the heating process used to kill Leeuwenhoek's tiny *animalcula* found in milk. The twentieth century heralded a very brave new medical world.

The carnage of World War I and the 1918 influenza pandemic cut short the celebrations. The morbidity rate from bacterially infected war wounds was high, often fatal, and the mortality rate from the Spanish flu eclipsed even that resulting from the war. By the 1930s, discoveries made in industrial chemical plants had cross-pollinated and encouraged the nascent pharmaceutical industry: an early example is the emergence of the antibacterial sulfa drugs, rooted in the chemical dye industry. The giant German chemical conglomerate I.G. Farben first synthesized and patented sulfa in 1906 as an ingredient in dye making. By the late 1930s, sulfa's newly appreciated antibacterial properties and lapsed original patent meant a frenzied free market—an unregulated opportunity for anyone who wanted to produce sulfa for medical use, with disastrous results for some.

The tale of the Elixir Sulfanilamide Disaster of 1937 presages the abuse of wonder drugs and underscores the adage that a little knowledge can be a dangerous thing. Prior to the wonders of penicillin, sulfa drugs were the first and only line of defense against infection. World War II newsreels or battlefield dramas frequently show a medic liberally sprinkling a powdery substance on a fallen soldier's wound. On the real battlefield, it was sulfa in powdered form, and it saved lives. Back in 1936, sulfa was manufactured as a powder or in tablet form. In order to sell as an easy-to-swallow liquid, in "elixir" form, the sulfa had to be dissolved. The Massengill Company used diethylene glycol as a solvent, a compound sometimes found in antifreeze that is poisonous to humans and animals. The toxic medicine was flavored with raspberry syrup, and sold to people of all ages, for a wide variety of ailments: children got it for sore throats; adults took it for gonorrhea. Over one hundred people died and the 1938 Federal Food, Drug, and Cosmetic Act was passed in response to the tragedy.

Alexander Fleming was the first to note that certain cultures of "germs" (a strain of *Staphylococcus* bacteria) avoided growing into a region of a petri dish "contaminated" by a naturally occurring mold in Fleming's none-too-sterile lab. Further study confirmed this was penicillin—the first naturally occurring antibiotic.

It took from 1928, when Fleming first identified penicillin, until 1941 when it was first used on a human patient, Constable Albert Alexander, a London policeman. A scratch on his face, initially ignored, resulted in both staphylococcal and streptococcal infections. His head became a mass of abscesses to the extent that doctors had been forced to remove one of his eyes. Sulpha drugs were applied without success. He was considered terminal when his case came to the attention of Howard Florey, the chemist who first succeeded in extracting penicillin in quantity. Starting February 12, 1941, the dying patient received two hundred milligrams of penicillin in an IV drip. Doctors concerned about possible side effects were afraid to give him more, and in truth, there wasn't that much available to begin with. However, the patient as guinea pig showed immediate improvement: his fever dropped; his appetite returned; his wounds appeared to be healing. But the supply of penicillin was exhausted after five days, even including small, recycled amounts extracted from Alexander's urine. Ten days later, on March 15, 1941, he suffered a relapse and died.

Even as chemists mastered the tricks to produce penicillin in reliably adequate dosages, the bacteria *Staphylococcus aureus* was acquiring the ability to overcome the threat of the wonder drug. Select strains of the bacteria became resistant because they were able to produce penicillinase, an enzyme that destroys penicillin. Such resistance was noticed as early as 1942 and by 1947 had spread to the point where nearly forty percent of *S. aureus* strains isolated in one British hospital were penicillin resistant. What was needed was a wonder drug that would kill penicillin-resistant *S. aureus*, and what Beecham Research Laboratories came up with in 1959 was BRL 1241, a chemical derivative of penicillin later known as methicillin.

Hopes were high for methicillin's toxic effects on staph infections because as a synthetic compound, it was unlikely that methicillin would be destroyed by a bacterial enzyme.

The logic was impeccable—but only if the destruction of penicillin by penicillinase was the sole way a staphylococcus could become penicillin resistant. It was not.

Bacteria, like other living things, are cell based. For bacteria, a single cell suffices. Cell walls are built by enzymes, a cell's go-to team for everything from metabolism to waste removal to defense. Enzymes are produced according to coding instructions carried in the bacterial DNA. Destroy the cell wall, destroy that bacteria's life. Penicillin, at least with those bacteria that are not resistant to it, binds to and prevents enzymes from building the crucial cell wall. But what if the bacteria acquired a gene that coded for a different enzyme, an enzyme that was not inhibited by penicillin? It wouldn't matter that the bacteria couldn't produce an enzyme to destroy the penicillin first. The bacteria would survive unscathed because the new enzyme would not be hindered from building the bacteria's protective cell wall.

Fleming cautioned his contemporaries not to overuse penicillin: if too little were used, or too much, it would result in bacterial resistance to the antibiotic.[3] What he could not have known was that sequences of bacterial DNA already existed that could confer resistance to molecules of antibiotics. Contacts (and consequent adaptations) between bacteria and the molds that produce molecules of penicillin had been neighbors in the soil for millennia, mindlessly exchanging bits of their DNA with the help of plasmids, peculiar circular pieces of DNA usually found in bacterial cells. What was needed to produce a super resistant bacteria was a massive challenge—something that would wipe out those bacterial strains carrying little or no genetically resistant DNA sequences, leaving the survivors of such a battle to multiply with most of the competition killed off—a stimulating if dangerous environment was called for, one where failure to overcome the challenges meant death, but success meant a pathogen few, if any, antibiotics could stop. Antibiotics offer the environmental stimulus and represent the challenge to overcome—in effect, they provide a bacterial Everest, something to separate those strains genetically able to overcome the antibiotic onslaught and reach the top (i.e., survive) from those which, lacking the necessary genetic resistance, are killed by coming into contact with the antibiotic molecular "mountain."

Poor Constable Alexander—his doctors struggled to produce enough penicillin to knock off his staphloccocus infection. They didn't succeed for Alexander, but their efforts contributed to *S. aureus*'s resistance by providing it a richer than usual antibiotic environment. In evolutionary terms, it was a hard sweep, a genetic adaptation attributable to a single gene or small sequence of DNA code.

Like all bacteria, methycillin-resistant *Staphylococcus aureus* (MRSA) are capable of multiplying rapidly, and in favorable conditions, their numbers increase exponentially. Since 1961 when MRSA was first discovered in a hospital in UK, many different strains have acquired resistance. Conditions for MRSA's spread have grown increasingly favorable, correlating positively with the increase in agricultural practices that keep animals confined in highly concentrated populations, subject to immunological stress and awash in antibiotics given to offset the damage such concentrations ensure.

It might seem to an alien observer that we are consciously following a recipe for the creation of superbugs. CAFOs are our mixing bowls. Boils and carbuncles with a side of *Salmonella*: take a pinch of the genetic code that confers antibiotic resistance from any bovine or porcine pathogenic bacteria; transfer it to a nearby infectious but not necessarily antibiotic-resistant strain of a human bacteria. Let replicate. Serve at your own risk.

MRSA's favored accommodations in humans and farmed animals are warm, moist, nasal passages. Hand to nose to udder to nose. So it goes. Co-infection can move in either direction, from human to animal and vice versa. Cue the violins for a romantic moment of contact between a pig MRSA and a human MRSA. The horizontal gene transfer mambo! Pig MRSA incorporates genes from human MRSA (or vice versa), increasing MRSA's pathogenicity, that is, MRSA's ability to successfully infect an organism it didn't infect before the transfer dance. Having a fresh host to infect improves the chances of survival for this mixed-gene menace.

Strains of MRSA are classified as one of two general types: hospital acquired and community acquired. Community acquisition is defined in the negative sense, i.e., infection found in individuals who have not been hospitalized or undergone minor surgical treatments such as dialysis in at least one year. Potential community membership is broad and covers all ages: scout troops, sports teams, and elderly residents of nursing homes. With the rise of concentrated animal feeding organizations, workers have been infected who tend the meat supply either before or after slaughter. The community member frequently associated with maintaining a reservoir of MRSA is now a production unit formerly known as a hog, chicken, turkey, or dairy cow.

MRSA may have first evolved in a hospital setting, but it found an even more compatible home on the industrial dairy farm, where conditions are optimal for MRSA to evolve and thrive. To become drug-resistant, the *S. aureus* bacteria need a location in which to grow (something to infect): the bovine udder is made to order. Enter the industrialized, high stress, growth-hormone and antibiotic-drug-abusing corporate factory farm. As early as 1946, antibiotics were administered to dairy cattle with mastitis, an infection of the udder. Infection is unavoidable due to the excessive stress and demands placed on the metabolism of every bovine production unit. Near constant pregnancy and simultaneous lactation erode the animal's natural immunities and foster the development of chronic, subclinical mastitis. To reduce the severity of infections promoted by industrial-strength husbandry practices, the factory farm manager provides an ill-considered delivery of antibiotics to all production units, whether or not infection is present. The certainty of infections and the use of various drugs to keep milk production profitably high and milk contamination acceptably low, constitute the cost of doing business. Along with feed and the electric power to run the milking machines, the drug bill must also be paid. Severely infected cows are culled, not cured.

What this means for the average dairy cow is best illustrated by her life cycle. She is born and immediately orphaned, although her mother may still be alive. Mother and baby are kept apart for two reasons: (1) thanks to her mother's unnatural diet of protein supplements and grains, the milk produced proves too rich to be easily digestible, and (2) allowing a bond to form between mother and daughter only makes the inevitable separation that much harder. The baby will be hand-fed calf starter, a commercial nutrient, until her digestive system matures to the point where she can handle solids (in dairy cattle, anywhere between three and eight weeks). If the calf is male, his fate is sooner sealed: slaughtered at three weeks for so-called "bob veal" or crated, protein deprived, and slaughtered at eighteen weeks. His sister will be sexually mature at seven to eight months of age, and artificially inseminated a few months after her first birthday. The food provided the calf up to this point is an investment in future production profits. If for some reason she fails to become pregnant, she will be slaughtered. Cows who don't give milk are as useless on a dairy farm as their brothers.

If the insemination succeeds, she will be pregnant approximately 281 days, slightly longer than humans, whose babies are considered full term at 270 days. Like her mother, she will give birth, and not be allowed to nurse or bond with her calf. She is now a milk producer, and for the first time in her two years of life, she is earning her keep. Another six to eight weeks will pass and a second insemination will be attempted.

She has now graduated from heifer status to full-fledged cow; her body is multitasking, producing milk for the long-gone first calf while she carries a second calf to term. She will produce milk until a few weeks prior to this second birth, when she will be artificially dried off with still more antibiotics. After another postpartum rest period of six to eight weeks, during which time she is producing milk but not pregnant, she will be inseminated for the third time, and so goes the unremitting lactation cycle. Each successive lactation period causes unrelenting stress on the cow's metabolism to sustain simultaneous lactation and pregnancy. With each successive pregnancy, her productivity drops, as measured in gallons of milk collected. Once she no longer produces the quantities of milk that justify the expense of her keep, she is sent to slaughter.

Careful records are kept. The dairy corporation must balance the amount of milk a cow produces against the severity of her mastitis. A cow with mastitis will give less milk, and the Somatic Cell Count (SCC—the amount of pathogens and antibiotic residue contaminating the milk) will be higher in her milk than in a healthier animal. A certain amount of contamination in raw milk is legally acceptable. The level of contamination is not necessarily assessed for each individual cow, but rather on the contents of the holding

tank, where the milk from all the cows is combined. The source of the elevated cell count can be an infection from contagious bacteria like *S. aureus* or contamination with *Salmonella* or *E. coli* as a result of unsanitary milking practices.

To meet demand, meaning the profit margin, the bottom line of a dairy operation, the focus is not on keeping the cud-chewing production units in good working order. Here, the milk-making machines are meant to be worked to death, kept on only so long as they meet production quotas, even as the stress of constant producing quickly breaks them down, which is why the average dairy cow who might live and produce milk twenty or more years if turned out in a sympathetic pasture, is sent to slaughter after two or three births when she is between four and five years of age. Cows living in so-called sustainable organic dairy herds live healthier lives on grass rather than concrete. They are milked twice a day, not three times, and their feed, and consequently their milk and flesh, is free of hormones and antibiotics. But like their corporate cow sisters, they are impregnated annually, and still deprived of nursing their own calves. The organic farmer makes a Faustian bargain: because of the reduced stress and the acceptance of lower yields by the farmer, these "sustainable" cows can last eight to ten years before being sent to slaughter.

Meanwhile, MRSA has found pleasant accommodation in the nasal passages of both farm animals and humans. Even if the cow or hog is not a direct reservoir of MRSA, the animals can be a reservoir of antibiotic-resistant genes that can then be transferred to human pathogens. Co-infection (infection in either direction, from human to animal and vice versa) is a problem since it can put an animal pathogen, one that does not cause disease in humans, in proximity to another disease agent that might then develop the ability to infect both human and animal hosts. Under these conditions there is a greater opportunity for animal and human pathogens to meet and exchange genetic information.

NOTES

1. Walt Kelly, *The Pogo Papers*, William Konecky Associates, Inc., 1952.

2. The grim images Dickens drew accurately reflected the condition of the food supply in Victorian England. In addition to mineral poisonings from food containers and water pipes, ". . . the deliberate adulteration of food was a common and, until 1860, a virtually unrestricted practice . . . An 1863 report to the Privy Council stated that one-fifth of the meat sold came from diseased cattle."
Bruce Haley. *The Healthy Body and Victorian Culture*. Cambridge, MA: Harvard University Press, 1978, as cited by "Health and Hygiene in the Nineteenth Century."
http://www.victorianweb.org/science/health/health10.html

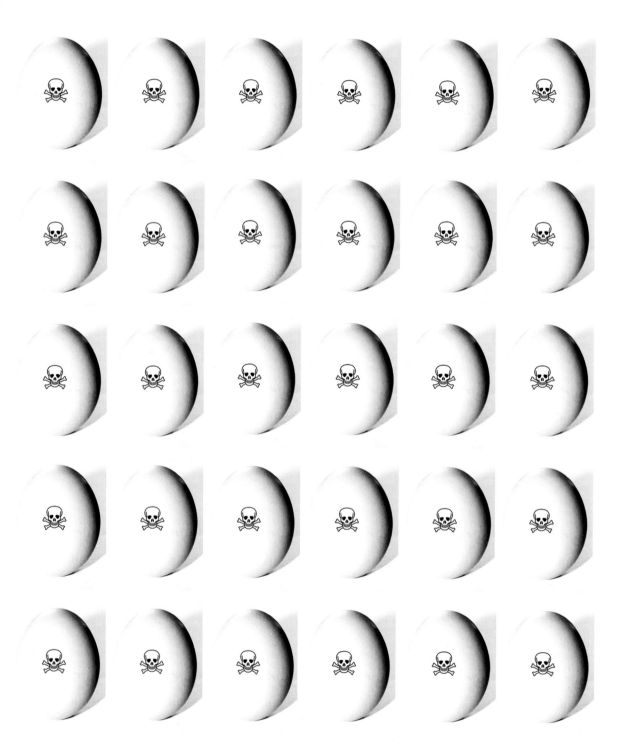

THE JOURNAL OF
EMERGING (AND RE-EMERGING)
INFECTIOUS DISEASES

The supposed Golden Age of Medicine in the 1950s and 1960s quickly turned out to be fool's gold. Still, given the evidence of those days, the notion of having reached a medical Millennium was not unreasonable. Yet fifty years later, there are now enough emerging infectious diseases to merit a scientific journal devoted solely to their study. Since 1995, *The Journal of Emerging Infectious Diseases* has published research on pathogens that first began to appear as significant blips on public health radar during the 1970s and '80s: Campylobacter, Ebola hemorrhagic fever, Hantavirus, HIV/AIDS, Legionnaires' disease, Lyme disease, Mad Cow, SARS, West Nile virus, not to mention resurgent tuberculosis and a plague of antibiotic-resistant microbes. Factors contributing to these emerging infections can often be traced back to changes in the scale and methods for how food animals are reared and slaughtered. Additionally, no place on the planet is now truly remote from human population centers, and the migration time for people and pathogens between one place and any other has been cut to hours rather than weeks or months.

Fleming, Koch, Lister, Pasteur, Salk, Sabin, and the other giants of nineteenth- and twentieth-century medicine, who helped defeat old style infectious diseases would be amazed, and no doubt, depressed, but if the scientific ego has been every so slightly crushed by the resurgence of old infectious diseases, or the emergence of new ones, fortunately deeper understandings have evolved that restore enthusiasm for investigation.

Genetics and biochemistry have broadened our appreciation for the marvelous mysteries that constitute how living things manage their affairs. We now know that genetic material can be and frequently is transferred horizontally, that is, from one species or strain of bacteria to another. As a process, horizontal gene transfer is quite ancient, but it came as breaking news to mid-twentieth-century biology, relative to the more familiar vertical gene transfer (as the method of reproduction for birds, bees, and people is commonly understood). In fact, horizontal gene transfer may be the fastest and most direct way to bring about a major change in the biology of a pathogen with respect to its ability to cause infectious disease or defend against cellular damage when dosed with an antibiotic. What allows horizontal gene transfer to take place?

The workhorse that makes horizontal gene transfer possible is a DNA molecule, first termed a "plasmid" by Nobel laureate Joshua Lederberg in 1952. Plasmids are circular rings of DNA that can be transferred, from one cell to another, but like viruses, plasmids don't exist or reproduce as independent cells or organisms. Finding a place for plasmids along the continuum from what is life to what is not life is tricky: like viruses, they hover in a twilight zone, neither living nor lifeless, because despite carrying chunks of the genetic material of life, they don't have all the component parts to reproduce independently. Instead, in order to get around, plasmids must rely on bacterial host cells. Plasmid DNA can integrate with a bacteria's chromosomal DNA, and be inherited by the next bacterial generation. But the plasmid can also transfer its DNA directly from one species of bacteria to another. In this way, plasmids can pick up and pass along the genetic ability for bacteria to become increasingly virulent and/or resist antibiotics. This was the case with the appearance of the enzyme penicillinase, the first known bacterial countermove to the antimicrobial power of penicillin. Before plasmids had even been discovered, the ability to make a penicillin-digesting enzyme was transferred between and among different strains of bacteria by plasmids, years ahead of Lederberg's identification of plasmids and their role as vectors. The result of these transfers, like the process itself, is haphazard and unpredictable, but such is the modest genius of evolution—a process that does not demand or expect perfection; where success is measured in survivability, and nothing more.

Bacteria with their hitchhiking plasmids are certainly plentiful. As a group, the prokaryotes make up most of the biomass on the planet, and on a personal note, a humbling ninety percent of all human bodies. Yet our species continues to influence microbial life out of all proportion to our numbers. Unfortunately, the outcomes of our unthinking interventions with the animals we hunt or domesticate and raise often mean new diseases and/or environmental damage.

Zoonotic pathogens, that is, organisms causing diseases in animals, are microscopic, if mindless, entrepreneurs. They exploit chance opportunities to move in and mine the resources of previously untapped regions of their universe. We encourage and enlarge the pandemic possibilities by fostering conditions where, as we have seen, bacteria from different species can come into contact with one another, and via plasmid exchange, do the DNA transfer dance. Viruses too, can cross the species barrier and exchange DNA, without the help of plasmid dance partners.

It is only a question of time before the next bird flu pandemic arrives. When wild birds stop over in parts of China and Southeast Asia on their annual migrations, they feed, rest, and certainly poop on the land and waters where, for thousands of years, individual farmers have kept both domesticated fowl and pigs. The region's live-animal markets present an opportunity for pathogens from different species to meet and exchange DNA. Introduce the unsanitary, high stress living conditions for factory-farmed chickens, a late twentieth-century agribusiness import to the region, and the viral mixing goes into overdrive.

The result? An influenza accident waiting to happen. The H5N1 virus signaled its appearance in Hong Kong in 1997, and has since made its way into dozens of countries, infected millions of birds, and threatens to trigger a human catastrophe.[1]

Sometime in the last 150 years, a virulent strain of immunodeficiency virus jumped to humans from chimpanzees that were already carrying a version of a simian immunodeficiency virus. The SIV in those chimpanzees was the result of another, even earlier species jump into chimpanzees from SIVs found in two different monkey species. The dual-source SIV is believed to have hybridized in chimpanzees to a third form of SIV that had the potential to infect both chimpanzees and humans. We unleashed an eventual epidemic of HIV/AIDS when this virulent chimpanzee SIV infected its first human hosts, most likely as a result of humans eating or butchering bushmeat. Not surprisingly, it is suggested that the chimpanzees contracted their SIV the same way, by hunting and eating monkeys that carried their own versions of SIV. Until that most recent jump, chimpanzees were the quiescent, otherwise healthy, formerly remote reservoirs for HIV.[2]

In the North Carolina Neuse River basin, the largest fish kill on any North American river occurred in 1991. Over five days, a billion menhaden died. Many were washed ashore along the tidal river's banks. Menhaden are small, herring-like, oily ocean-dwelling fish. They constitute an ecological foundation species: as filter feeders, they turn the sun's energy stored in the algae and other vegetation they consume into protein, which then is available to feed larger carnivorous fish. They are commercially valuable as feed for poultry, swine, and farmed fish when rendered into fishmeal. Their contribution to the human food supply is thus indirect: they are used as bait by commercial and recreational fishermen, or processed into omega-3 oils. Adults deposit their larvae in the ocean close to tidal river outlets that then wash the fish-to-be up into estuaries where they eventually find their way even further up the rivers and streams to hatch. At this point, the young fish are called "peanuts." After about a year, the peanuts are ready to return to the ocean and what will be their adult lives. It was these migrating peanuts, heading down the river and out to sea, that died.

Suspected in the disaster was the nitrogen- (in the form of ammonia) and phosphorous-rich runoff from lagoons of spilled pork poop, the fecal output of the countless factory farms raising hogs in confinement. Duplin County in North Carolina has the highest concentration of pigs per acre in the world. At any given moment, there are ten million pigs being raised in the state and each farm produces the waste of a city of twenty thousand people. Unlike the sewage from twenty thousand humans, when pigs produce it, no one is held responsible for its safe disposal and no regulations demand that it be treated. Had the sewage killed the fish and if so, how? Did it deplete the river of oxygen, leaving the fish to suffocate? The sewage played a crucial part in the fish kill, but the main culprit was an odd, recently discovered microscopic critter—part plant, part animal; sometime photosynthesizer, sometime vegetarian, sometime carnivore—*Pfiesteria piscicida*, named in honor of Lois Pfiester for her work with algae, the vegetable part of Pfiesteria's diet. Pfiesteria is a dinoflagellate ("whirling whip") with a complex life cycle that includes taking different forms at different stages, depending on conditions in its environment. It can remain dormant for years, encased as a cyst on the riverbed until conditions are favorable for it to wake up and start feeding. In its mobile form, it gets around gondolier-style, as the phylum name suggests, by whirling (dino) a single whiplike oar (flagella). The sewage pollution, like the proverbial ill wind, initially did the Pfiesteria lots of good, because the nutrient runoff promoted the growth of algae. Peanuts also thrive on algae. For a time, it was a banquet for the Menhaden peanuts and Pfiesteria alike, until the excreta from the peanut fish triggered a change in the Pfiesteria—they began to secrete a neurotoxin. The fish were stunned, leaving them easy prey to slow suffocation from partial paralysis that both prevented their escape and impaired their breathing. At the same time, the Pfiesteria abandoned their vegetarian ways and began nibbling at the stunned, already dying fish. The raw, circular lesions on countless bodies of dead Menhaden peanuts was compelling evidence for this hypothesis.

Biologists first became aware of Pfiesteria in 1988 when the veterinary department of North Carolina State University put fish in an aquarium filled with water from the nearby Pamlico River. When the fish unexpectedly died, biologists sought an explanation and found the answer in the toxic microscopic protozoan in the water. Pfiesteria's full name translates as "Pfiester's fish killer." The massive fish kills some years later produced evidence of Pfiesteria along with the algal blooms, and this led investigators to suspect Pfiesteria's involvement. Pfiesteria's toxin causes neurological anomalies in humans (mood swings, memory loss) and to paralysis in small fish, leading to suffocation. The CDC has declared Pfiesteria may be studied only using biosafety level 3 precautions, the same level of safety demanded when studying HIV.

Massive fish kills in the presence of Pfiesteria have since been recorded in the Chesapeake Bay region, where chicken waste from factory farms and processing plants provide their share of the nutrient pollution that feeds Pfiesteria and kills the fish.

The Fore tribespeople in New Guinea called it kuru for the uncontrollable shaking seen in the people infected with it. Neurological impairments of speech and thought were also evident. In the western world, the symptoms of late-stage CJD (Creutzfeldt-Jakob disease) are similar (shaking, dementia). There is no cure. Death comes anywhere from four months to a little over a year from the onset of symptoms, though it may take decades before any symptoms appear. Autopsies reveal brains that look more like sponges, and thus the name for this kind of disease: spongiform encephalopathies. BSE is its bovine form.

BSE is one reason why a cow may be a "downer," an animal unable to get up or walk on her own into the slaughterhouse. The press in England gave it a snappier name: Mad Cow Disease. Mink on fur farms and European felines have their own versions of spongy brain degeneration (MSE and FSE). Sheep develop "scrapie," similar to a Chronic Wasting Disease that infects deer and elk. Whatever the name, the infectious agent is not a bacteria, a virus, or any kind of protozoan. It is an unusually hardy, hard to destroy protein termed a prion found in neurological tissues (brain, nerves, spinal cord). Stanley Prusiner postulated and named the prion based on his understanding of it as a protein that could possess infectious qualities. Smaller than a virus, prions are misfolded proteins that cause cell damage by causing other normally folded proteins to misfold. The damaged cells are then unable to protect themselves from further damage or activate any of the cell's repair mechanisms. Prusiner's work in the early 1980s, positing this previously unheard of bit of protein, met rabid skepticism at the time. In 1997, he received the Nobel Prize in Medicine for his studies of infectious prions.

Kuru, CJD, BSE, scrapie, and any other spongiform encephalopathies arise when infectious prions from neurological tissue are incorporated into the body of a human, cow, sheep, goat, mink, or other animal. The easiest way to do this is by eating the infected tissue. The Fore prepared and ritualistically ate the brains of dead relatives and contracted kuru. In a very few cases found in modern hospitals, corneal transplants infected recipients with a form of CJD. Sheep in Scottish meadows came down with scrapie after eating the remains of elk or deer that died from a neurological wasting disease. Pet foods and protein feeds for poultry, pigs, and cattle include meat byproducts, which includes spinal cords, brains, and nerve tissue. The human or animal food supply may still include downer cows, or cows where the disease is still incubating and does not manifest any symptoms prior to slaughter.

When prion-infested tissues are transmitted from one animal to another, the prions go along, unchanged and unimpaired in their ability to produce neurological damage. Prions cannot be killed because they are not, strictly speaking, alive. The normal preparation of meat doesn't destroy them. Bleach will destroy them, but human beings do not knowingly or legally wash their meat with bleach. Sterilization in an autoclave will also destroy prions, along with any taste and texture the meat may have had. You would be correct if you thought CJD could be avoided by not eating brains or spinal cord tissue. The problem is, sometimes prion-infected neurological tissue gets into the food supply, most easily in the form of hot dogs and other processed meats.

Processed meats are made from so-called "recovered" or "reclaimed meat"—a slurry or paste of scraps and bits that are left over after the majority of the carcass has been separated from the bone and divided by hand into commercial grade cuts. The most efficient, least wasteful way to get at these last bits of usable flesh is not by hand slicing but rather by using increasingly sophisticated mechanical means. Mechanically separated meat (MSM) and advanced meat recovery (AMR) systems continue the philosophy of the nineteenth-century Chicago meatpackers' boast to use everything but the squeal. Unfortunately, occasional bits of spinal cord or other neural tissue may be incorporated accidentally. If the animal was infected with disease-producing prions, the prions will be there, ready to infect whoever eats the hot dog that included these scrapings.

In an attempt to discover a process that would render the prion harmless, and still leave the meat edible, food engineers "prepared a paste of scrapie prion-infected hamster brain tissue mixed with hot dogs." This bizarre, potentially lethal concoction was heated to 250–275 degrees Fahrenheit and subjected to "short bursts of ultra high pressure, in excess of 100,000 lbs. per square inch." The engineers found that they were able to retain the basic texture and flavor of the processed meat while reducing the prions to non-infective levels.[3]

NOTES

1. Kennedy Shortridge, Introduction to *Bird Flu: A Virus of Our Own Hatching*, by Michael Greger. http://birdfluebook.com/a.php?id=2

2. Bailes et al. (2003) "Hybrid Origin of SIV in Chimpanzees", *Science*, vol. 300, p. 1713.
This article concludes that wild chimps had been infected simultaneously with two different simian immunodeficiency viruses which had "viral sex" to form a third virus that could be passed on to other chimps and, more significantly, was capable of infecting humans and causing AIDS. These two different viruses were traced back to a SIV that infected Red-capped Mangabeys and one found in greater spot-nosed monkeys. It is believed that the hybridization took place inside chimps that had become infected with both strains of SIV after they hunted and killed members of the two smaller species of monkey.

3. Paul Brown et al., "Pressure Combined with Heat Reduces Prion Infectivity in Processed Meats," press release, Monday, May 5, 2003. National Institute of Neurological Disorders and Stroke.
The combination of temperature and high pressure has been used commercially for the past fifteen years to reduce the amount of bacteria in foodstuffs and to preserve ham, chicken, salsa, and other foods. Brown said his team "took the process one step further, to see if it would kill prions, which it did." He called the discovery a relatively inexpensive, practical step to potentially improve the safety of processed meats.

THE FIRST ANIMAL FACTORY

1907: The Hen's Place on the Farm

The Kansas farmer, or the farmer in general, has not yet fully recognized the full value of poultry on the farm for supplying food for his table. Besides the eggs that they produce, which are being recognized as one of the most wholesome food products that we have, the poultry should furnish to the farmer the bulk of his meat for the year, which can be had at all times in a fresh and healthy condition. There is no other meat that can be produced as cheaply and is as wholesome and digestible according to the chemist's analysis.[1]

As the 1907 bulletin from the Kansas State Agricultural College describes, and as was the case until the 1920s, the casual pace of farm life for a chicken consisted of looking out for the fox, the freedom to scratch and wander around the yard for grit and insects, and to savor vegetable peels and corn meal sprinkled by the farmer's wife—it represented a bucolic scene, at least during warmer weather and longer daylight hours. Winters meant egg production dropped off even as chickens ran up the farmers' feed bills during the cold months when they couldn't regularly get outside the barn to scratch for bugs. The discovery in the 1920s of vitamin D supplements meant chickens could be kept indoors, at lower cost, all year round.

"Cheap, wholesome and digestible," the farm bulletin enthused in 1907. These traits made chickens the ideal candidates for the first factory farms, where economies of scale promoted a standardized, controlled environment, lower labor costs, and higher profits. The new technologies ensured more abundant and less-expensive food: in a 1928 presidential campaign speech, Herbert Hoover promised "a chicken in every pot and a car in every garage." It took FDR, the New Deal, and the economic lessons of World War II to fulfill much of Hoover's promised prosperity, but by the 1950s and '60s, more chickens were in more pots than ever before.

But "plenty" had its drawbacks for both the farmers and the hens. Prices dropped; chickens and eggs lost their status as luxury foods. The lower prices increased demand. To keep income steady, the volume of sales had to increase, which meant higher production quotas for chickens and eggs. Farmers were encouraged to increase the size of their flocks, and that meant cramming more chickens into the existing space. Cage occupancy rates doubled and tripled, and the crowding continued. Floors in the broiler sheds were wall to wall with birds. Breeding programs standardized "heirloom" chickens, which once had been the source of both eggs and meat, into two distinct versions: layers and broilers. Chicken temperament was less easily standardized. Personalities could not be bred to accept overcrowding with equanimity.

If you were to graph across time, from 1907 to the present, the inexorable reduction of space that each chicken is allotted against the dwindling number of family farms, the two curves would fairly well match, both careening downhill. In 1907, a chicken was thought to need five square feet of space. Today, hobbyists who want to raise chickens are advised to allow four square feet per bird when figuring out the size of a chicken coop—even three square feet will do in a pinch, but hobbyists are cautioned that the chickens may feel stressed with anything smaller. Currently, a commercially held battery hen's share of her cage is smaller than a sheet of copy paper, slightly more than one-half of one square foot.

Corporate poultry producers sear or otherwise clip the beaks of young chicks. The stress of overcrowding will have the densely packed birds pecking at one another in a futile attempt to find a non-existent comfort zone. A dull beak does less damage than a sharp one. Stress upon stress is laid on these birds: unnaturally rapid growth, fecal dust and ammonia in the air and in their lungs, and shoulder-to-shoulder overcrowding. Despite supplements of the "sunshine" vitamin, these birds never know the warmth or light of the sun. These psychological and physical stresses cause a fight-or-flight response in the birds, despite the fact that neither tactic will resolve the stress they feel. In response to an impossible situation, their bodies secrete adrenaline, a hormone produced by the enteric nervous system, the same system that sends butterflies to human stomachs in times of stress.

The field of microbial endocrinology studies the effects of stress hormones on pathogenic organisms. Stress hormones produced by the corporately farmed chicken ironically make bacterial pathogens more effective at infection. In the case of campylobacter, the animal's stress hormones trigger conditions that lead to an increase in bacterial virulence. Campylobacter normally inhabits the intestinal tract, where it is subject to destruction by acidic digestive juices. In the presence of stress hormones, selection pressures kick in. Those bacteria that are better able to escape the acids and environmental conditions of the gut by passing through the intestinal wall will be the ones to survive and pass on their escapist skills to a new and more virulent generation. They reach the relative safety of muscle and organ tissues, where they remain until killed by adequate heat during cooking. The USDA reports campylobacter can be found in almost all raw poultry. Appropriate cautions to avoid contamination for those who slaughter and prepare poultry are ignored at the risk of food poisoning and death.

Another species of bacteria that infects chickens is *Salmonella*. Unfortunately, infected eggs give no hint of their toxicity. There is no outward sign that the laying hens harbor the disease. When tracing back the causes for the most recent *Salmonella* outbreak and the consequent recall of hundreds of millions of eggs, rats stand accused as carriers of the virulent bacteria. Rats and *Salmonella* go back a long way. In the late nineteenth century, a particular strain, *S. Typhimurium*, was found to be lethal in a colony of laboratory mice. Logic suggested *Salmonella* would be a good candidate to use as a weapon in the "War on Rats," waged in San Francisco in the early twentieth century. That international port city experienced occasional outbreaks of bubonic plague and cholera brought in by rats from the cargo ships. *Salmonella* didn't prove effective at eliminating the rats, but it did sicken and kill human beings who handled it. Yet *Salmonella* remained an ingredient in rat poison. In 1918, two people died and about thirty-five others were made ill after eating cake that had been intentionally poisoned with Ratin, a commercially available *Salmonella*-laced rat poison. The *Typhimurium* strain was found to be identical to strains known to contaminate meat. Rat poison manufacturers, apparently either unaware or indifferent to evidence that the rats were not affected by the *Salmonella*, switched to a different *Salmonella* strain, *Enteritidis*, and this too proved toxic to humans. Between 1920 and the 1940s, numerous outbreaks of accidental human poisonings were reported, including deaths, from *S. Enteritidis*–laced rodenticides.

Ratin continued to be used as rat poison in Europe until the 1960s, despite World Health Organization's recommendations against it. One unintended consequence of feeding rats *Salmonella* may have been the increase in *Salmonella* bacteria now carried by rats, thereby increasing the potential spread of the disease into the human food supply. Eggs, grains, milk, and meat may become contaminated by contact with rat feces in the environment. If a chicken ingests the bacteria, it can infect her ovaries and her eggs before they are laid. No external indication of infection will show up. The laying hen becomes a feathered Typhoid Mary (Mary Mallon, a cook and carrier of typhoid fever who infected dozens with the deadly disease in the early twentieth century).

The WHO ban on Ratin notwithstanding, a newer rodenticide, trade name Biorat, uses the same *S. Enteritidis* virulent strain of *Salmonella* as Ratin. Biorat is currently on sale in parts of Central and South America and Vietnam; its website (http://vietintelligence.com/bioratvn/sub.php?/=biorat) and advertising materials claim that Biorat is safe for humans. But Biorat is effective at killing rodents because it uses warfarin, a chemical that prevents blood from clotting. Rats that ingest Biorat hemorrhage to death. The added *Salmonella* does nothing to increase Biorat's rodent-killing effectiveness; on the contrary, the *Salmonella* presents an ongoing public health menace to humans.

Escherichia coli is the long-form name of an intestinal-dwelling species of bacteria named after its discoverer, the German pediatrician Theodor Escherich, who discovered it in 1885. Some *E. coli* strains are beneficial to have as residents of our guts. They produce vitamin K2, and like a vigilant neighborhood watch, *E. coli* discourage the successful colonization of other less benign bacteria on their home turf. But *E. coli* also comes in pathogenic strains and can be found in the tons of manure and animal waste sold for fertilizer, spilled into our waterways, or spread on fields of fruits and vegetables. When these toxins enter the food supply, outbreaks of severe diarrhea for adults, death for young children, the immune compromised, and the elderly follow too quickly for rescue by the recall of tainted meat, cookie dough, frozen pizza, lettuce, and spinach.

Cultures of *E. coli* are familiar subjects for study in biochemistry laboratories, and as a result, we know a little something about this particular prokaryote. Cattle and poultry may carry strains of *E. coli* that are virulent for humans, without becoming ill themselves. We promote the reproduction and survival of virulent *E. coli* by feeding cattle grain, rather than the grass or hay they have evolved to digest with greater ease. Switching grain-fed cows to a diet of hay for a few days before they are slaughtered seems to reduce the *E. coli* population. In grain-fed cattle, *E. coli* can develop resistance to destruction by stomach acids that otherwise would be fatal to most bacteria. The development of resistance is based on natural selection and evolution, the same process that has produced antibiotic-resistant bacteria and the more virulent forms of *Salmonella* and *Campylobacter*—"The process of natural selection allows organisms with the appropriate genes to survive and multiply where others cannot. Because cattle have been fed high-grain, growth-promoting diets for more than forty years . . . there has been ample opportunity to select acid-resistant forms."[2]

NOTES

1. "The Hen's Place on the Farm." Kansas State Agricultural College, Agricultural Experimentation Station, Bulletin 150, October 1907.

2. Jennifer Couzin, "Cattle Diet Linked to Bacterial Growth." *Science*, vol. 281, no. 5383, September 11, 1998, p. 1578.

3/28   An Unnatural Disaster, Croton Ohio   Sue Coe 01

Brave New Chicken

FISH STICKS

When our earliest ancestors hauled themselves out of the oceans to try their evolutionary luck on land, they left behind the ancestors of many of our marine cousins. And as is often the case with immigrants, some eventually thought better of life in the new lands and returned to the sea. Ample evidence of such treks exists in the fossil record and physiology of today's marine mammals—from sea to shore and back again, repeated at least seven times over hundreds of millions of years.

Almost alone among our cousins (with the exception of some social insects that practice, for want of a better word, either agriculture or manufacturing), we have developed land-based economies and practices reliant on taming, domesticating, or controlling the wild in order to move beyond subsistence hunting and gathering. Land-based agriculture revolutionized the human population's size, food supply, and economy. Industrial techniques and genetic engineering have added new chapters to that revolution's history, but until quite recently, the expectation was that fishing for food meant hunting for wild marine life in oceans or rivers, not harvesting them from where they were confined in conveniently located feedlots.

The wild doesn't easily bend toward either confinement or domestication. This is true for most animals, whether they live on land or in water. Wildness presents a problem for those who would farm the wild for crops of fish and fur. Naturally curious and frenetically mobile mink and fox remain wild when farmed (or "ranched"). Cooped up, unable to realize any normal physical and psychological needs, they grow stressed and fearful, driven to frenzied neurotic behaviors. They may develop stomach ulcers and often self-mutilate. Domestication of fur seals is a non-starter: there is no interest in figuring out how to run a fur farm nursery for baby seals, even if their fur is exceptionally warm, waterproof, and durable. Seals compete with the planet's top predator for fish, so hunting their babies for fur and flesh (a byproduct of the fur hunt) acts as a brake on seal populations, benefiting the human fishing fleet.

Which would bring us to a consideration of fish farming, or aquaculture, but we have gotten ahead of ourselves. Why the urge to farm fish? Why not just keep fishing the wild waters, as humans have done for millennia?

Time was, fresh fish were available only to those who lived close to the rivers or oceans where the fish lived and could be caught. Recall the truism about what becomes of fish and guests after three days, and appreciate the innovation salting fish meant in a world without refrigeration. Salted codfish kept remarkably well, and were palatable once re-soaked in fresh water. Caribbean slaves were kept alive and producing sugar cane, thanks to cheap, salted cod. The North Atlantic's fabled Grand Banks provided what appeared to be an endless supply. Cod were the ocean equivalent of the North American buffalo. Unlike the grazing, vegetarian buffalo, the cod were omnivorous predators, positioned, as the most successful predators inevitably are, near the top of complex food chains. By the 1950s, the health of the North Atlantic and the survival of its inhabitants, including the bounteous cod population, would be threatened by the introduction of refrigeration—specifically, the development of frozen foods for the market.

Refrigeration kept fish fresh by having them packed in ice rather than salt. The next logical step, freezing and packaging pre-cleaned, heat-it-and-eat-it fish, reduced meal preparation to opening a box. Cod was the first fish to be successfully marketed as frozen sticks. The public literally ate them up. Convenient to prepare and usually rectangular in shape, frozen foods brought about a paradigm change when it came to "mealtime." Fast foods and TV dinners filled the freezer bins in post-war "super" markets. Demand for a neighborhood fresh fishmonger plummeted but demand for frozen fish sticks soared.

To keep up with the increased demand meant larger fishing vessels, ocean-going assembly-line fish factories working around the clock, capable of processing one haul even as the nets were re-lowered to catch the next batch: "Tickler chains stir up the bottom, creating noise and dust. Cod, and other ground-fish, instinctively hide on the bottom when they sense danger, and the ticklers act like hunters beating bushes to drive birds out, sending the frightened cod out of their protective crannies and up into the nets. The ocean floor left behind is a desert" (Mark Kurlansky, *Cod*, p. 140).

The huge trawl nets snare everything in their path. Regulations to ensure a minimum opening size in the net's mesh, to allow smaller fish to escape, don't take into account the laws of physics. When smaller fish are swept into a net already filled with a solid wall of flesh and scales, there is no escape.

By the 1970s and '80s, scientists issued overfishing alerts, warning that fishing grounds were on the verge of collapse. The Atlantic cod off Newfoundland collapsed in 1992. The initial, shortsighted solution was to go fish somewhere else, like the Pacific, for something else, like pollack. But another response to the depletion of wild fish stocks was to find ways to grow and harvest them in captivity, which returns us to a consideration of aquaculture.

Wild animals that live their whole lives in water present unique problems for the budding marine aquaculturalist. Deciding to farm fish in tanks for market leaves plenty of room for mistakes, starting with the choice of fish one might seek to "industrialize."

Four of the most difficult species to try and adapt to confinement aquaculture are not, coincidentally, successful predators in their respective realms, and are increasingly the victims of overfishing: salmon, bass, cod, and tuna. As Paul Greenberg describes it, these same four fish represent an "epochal shift" across time as humans learned to exploit and expand human and marine geographic ranges, further and further out to sea. Historically, it began on land with easy access to rivers of salmon and trout. Then exploitation of fish resources moved to shallow waters off the coasts in a search for different species, often species of what we lump under the heading "bass." Further out, eventually to the edges of the continental shelf, the sailor-hunters chased cod, the fish that had fed Europe since the middle ages, and the earliest fish to be industrialized, and finally, in the deepest oceans, beyond international limits, what Greenberg calls "state-less fish"—including the majestic, warm-blooded, half-ton bluefin tuna.[1]

These four types of fish that have come to dominate the global fish market are poor choices for either hunting or domestication for a variety of reasons, but because their wild populations are increasingly endangered, the pressures only build to farm them, to try and make them "sustainable." This is a bad idea for a number of reasons.

Consider that "man does not select fish in the same way nature does" (Kurlansky, *Cod*, p. 196). The genetic characteristics including the reproductive fitness to pass along survival tested traits that may mean the difference between life and death in the wild are undetectable, extraneous, and unnecessary in a fish tank. A farmed fish with "poor foraging skills, clumsy when avoiding predators or with little resistance to disease" would not survive in the wild. "But it would survive in a pen, and if it had other characteristics that were particularly suited for farm life, the defective fish would flourish and possibly even dominate."

This can happen easily with so-called "ranched" salmon. Beginning and ending in fresh water with a saltwater sojourn in between, the wild salmon's life cycle is both dramatic and relatively amenable to human manipulation. The young in a freshwater stream that don't get gobbled up while either fertilized eggs or tiny "fingerlings," head for salt water after about a year and spend two to four years in the ocean, eating, escaping predators with teeth (or nets) until hormones beckon and they return to the waters of their birth to spawn and die. Once left free of their netting to feed and swim, the term "ranched" applies. Even better than ranched cattle, these fish, thanks to being imprinted on their home waters, actually round themselves up.

Humans play a part in selecting the mothers and fathers of the next fish generation. Eggs and sperm ("milt" in fish-speak) are manually harvested from likely looking females and males. In nature, these would be released and fertilized in a stream of water, outside the bodies of the parents. The fish farmer uses a bucket. In the process, the selected-for populations grow genetically more homogeneous and less diverse. This is the case with certain genetically modified salmon, bred to grow faster than their non-GMO age-mates. They grow quickly and become large enough to mate ahead of their non-GMO kin. In this sense, their speedier growth rate gives them a reproductive advantage, but their offspring are unfit for survival, whether from disease or predation, during that part of their life cycle when they aren't "protected" behind the factory doors. Breeding a homogeneous population ill-equipped to survive in the wild is a recipe for extinction. Keeping fish down on the farm that are otherwise unfit for life in the wild is not the answer either, since they don't necessarily stay put. Farmed fish are known to escape their pens and tanks and nets and interbreed with wild ones.

Assume for the moment that fish farming could overcome the genetic damage so easily and thoughtlessly inflicted on the schooling herds. The holy grail of fish farming, "sustainability," is the equilibrium between market demand for sushi, fish sticks, or shrimp cocktail and the harvesting of adequate numbers of marine lives to meet that demand, without driving species to extinction and destroying habitats and ecosystems in the process. Easier said than done.

Fishing for wild fish doesn't let up when fish are farmed. Aquaculture suggests a peculiarly circular definition of sustainability—avoid overfishing the wild by confining the wild, and doing their fishing for them. Having to catch two to four pounds of forage fish to yield one pound of farmed aquatic flesh for the human dinner plate is economically silly and strains the concept of "sustainable." It echoes the nonsense of feeding cattle less digestible, more expensive corn, when they have evolved to efficiently turn grass into muscle.

"Forage fish account for a staggering thirty-seven percent . . . of all fish taken from the world's oceans each year, and ninety percent of that catch is processed into fishmeal and fish oil. In 2002, forty-six percent of fishmeal and fish oil was used as feed for aquaculture . . ." ("Farm News" from TerraDaily.com).

Fish pellets already form a large part of the protein in industrialized hog (twenty-four percent) and poultry (twenty-two percent) diets, (not to mention the "animal by-products" listed on bags of dog and cat foods). Fish (and slaughterhouse) waste, whether poop or intestines, recirculates through the ponds, tanks, poultry sheds, hog houses, and cattle feedlots before coming to rest as shrink wrapped packages in grocery store coolers. Wild fish are more efficient hunters, without the wanton destruction and waste of by-catch. Sea birds and marine mammals lose to factory farms when forced to compete for forage fish.

Life on an industrial fish farm is not all that healthy for the scaled production units (ditto for industrialized farms growing creatures with fur, feathers, or hair). For starters, farmed predators fed fish pellets are not getting the necessary exercise needed to maintain health and fitness. Crowded and unsanitary conditions invite diseases and parasites. Illness in concentrated farmed populations easily spreads to wild populations. Farmed salmon are, well, sitting ducks, for infestation by sea lice. Where the commercial salmon nurseries grow, there too congregate colonies of sea lice, well situated to attack and injure wild salmon and kill the young ones in the netted farms that bobble at anchor in river deltas.

As with industrial farms on land, antibiotics for farmed fish are administered routinely—for protection against disease and parasites; to promote growth, and to bolster immune systems compromised by the stress of overcrowding. These antibiotic wastes add one more ingredient to an accumulating stew of pollution despoiling once clear waters: construction sediments and toxic run-off deplete the oxygen. Spills of radioactive water from nuclear power plants is now on the more familiar list of industrial-strength polluters: CAFOs (confined animal feeding operations), petro-chemical plants, deep water oil drilling, natural gas drilling ("fracking"), mining operations, and timber clear-cutting.

If, as some think, fish must be farmed in order to provide cheap sustainable protein supplies for humans, then some species of fresh water, vegetarian fish are better choices than larger marine predators like tuna and bass. Filter-feeding clams and oysters, wild or farmed, go finned fish one better: they can actually clean the waters in which they grow. But polyculture, the economic efficiency of having one species clean up and grow up on the fecal waste products of a different species does not confer immunity from diseases and parasites. Farming freshwater catfish and tilapia in polyculture makes economic sense in terms of what it costs to feed them, but both species are compromised from confinement stress and associated diseases.

Fish farming fosters an illusion of sustainability, overlooks the genetic, disease, and pollution problems and ignores the cruelties of the slaughtering process, visited upon all fish, whether farmed, ranched, or wild caught.

Fish certainly have the neural receptors to feel pain and react with stressful avoidance behaviors in response to fishhooks or injections of bee venom, as one experiment demonstrated (Sneddon, cited by Weis, p. 41). The ability to feel pain for any animal more complex than a sponge is essential. It can be a lifesaver. The argument goes that yes, fish feel something but their brains are not complex enough to interpret that as angst—as if that would make any difference, since the hogs and hens capable of angst-ridden neurosis are slaughtered with impunity. Time to rethink the meaning of "sustainable," and consider whether a sustainable, cruelty-free, pollution-free diet is possible.

As Michael Pollan suggests, omnivores do indeed have a dilemma. How to choose what to eat from among the wide variety of edibles offered by commerce and culture, sanctioned by habit and history, constrained by beliefs and budgets? Worse yet, how wise are such complicated choices when made in ignorance about the true cost of a calorie, both to the pocketbook and the planet?

The ocean's ecology, like that of the land, is a trickle up, down, and sideways recycling web of actions and interactions. Ecological richness defined by the coexistence of a wide variety of plant and animal lives in a particular environment is a balancing act; sustainability and equilibrium depend on avoiding overgrazing, overraising, and overhunting when it comes to who eats what and who or what gets eaten. For thousands of years before cod populations collapsed from over fishing, their immense numbers were self-sustained, even while satisfying the needs of their neighboring human populations around North Atlantic. In time, human populations exploded and the cod crashed.

Michael Pollan speaks of mutualism, of the mutual benefits given and received among different species coexisting in a particular habitat—think bees pollinating flowers. Everybody wins. In the wild, the Top Predator model is mutualistic. It describes the relationships between species that have evolved sustainable systems in many, if not all, ecological niches. Wolves in Yellowstone keep riverbanks from eroding by ensuring that young cottonwoods will not be nibbled to death by overgrazing, complacently munching elk herds. Plants, wolves, elk, and many other species thrive here because directly or indirectly, their neighborly sharing of the land and waters provides mutual benefits for all. Sharks along the Atlantic Coast of the United States keep the population of cownosed rays in check, ensuring the survival of shellfish that otherwise the rays would eat into oblivion. But these elemental realities of ecology were understood only after the fact; after the riverbanks eroded, the shellfish populations collapsed, and the environment grew less rich, less able to sustain life.

Ray Hilborn, a professor in aquatic sciences at the University of Washington, has suggested that if we eat less fish and impose a harvesting moratorium in an attempt to save the oceans "we will likely eat more beef, chicken, and pork. And the environmental costs of producing more livestock are much higher than accepting fewer fish in the ocean: lost habitat, the need for ever more water, pesticides, fertilizer and antibiotics, chemical runoff and 'dead zones' in the world's seas."[2] That is true, as far as it goes. But Hilborn offers only two options: either eat more fish and spare the flesh grown on land, or eat less fish, and watch bad stuff get worse. In his scenario, the fish to eat more of would be an abundant, kinder-to-the-environment fish. It would be an eco-rational choice of fish, one carefully caught if wild, or raised with less waste and pollution, less endangerment to fragile wild populations. Maybe clams and oysters that clean up waters others have dirtied? Alternatively, if clam chowder is rejected, then the expectation is even more pollution to land and water from land-based industrial flesh factories.

However, there is a third way: abstain from eating beef, chicken and pork and fish. Too soon? Too radical?

In theory, sustainable fishing methods make reasonable noises. Call this the "we can have our fish and eat it too" philosophy. Unfortunately, the plan on paper to reduce bycatch and pollution doesn't reflect the current state of lax, producer-friendly, uneven regulation, and lip service cooperation. In theory, international and regional stakeholders mandate and enforce a reduction in the catch of endangered species, like migratory shark and bluefin tuna. In practice, powerful political lobbies ensure continued human predation for corporate profit. This is rampant capitalism, high on social Darwinism and laboring under the misapprehension that our peculiar forms of predation are immune from ecological blowback. The warnings of marine biologists and ecologists are seen as alarmist rather than realistic. Skepticism too often out-polls science, resulting in the denial of the impact of human activity on climate. Irreversible climate change can alter the salinity and pH of the oceans, impacting all life, land, and sea. Current industrialized aquaculture practices do not foster a restoration of ecological balance. Equilibrium doesn't take well to tinkering although moratoriums have shown the resilience of living beings to swim, fly, and creep back from the edge of extinction.

Humans are the planet's apex predator. What threat will keep us, not unlike the elk in Yellowstone, from destroying our ecosystem, our planet? Who or what will serve as our mutualistic constraint? It won't be the wolves. Economically strapped fishermen are sailing longer hours, farther from their home ports, hunting deeper beneath the ocean waves and carrying higher operating costs just to stay even with what they earned a few decades ago. Fish farmers and ranchers in what is a field only one generation old or less, are making it up as they go along. The full impact of their activities is yet unknown. What we do know, however, is that the ocean from which all life on earth has grown, the ocean on which all life relies, is changing, and not for the better.

NOTES

1. Paul Greenberg, *Four Fish: The Future of the Last Wild Food*. New York, NY: Penguin Press, 2010.

2. Ray Hilborn, "Let Us Eat Fish." Op-Ed, *New York Times*, April 14, 2011.

REFERENCES

Bill Gifford, "Something Fishy in Washington." *Harper's* magazine, June 1996.

Paul Greenberg, "An Oyster on the Seder Plate?" Op-ed, *New York Times*, April 18, 2011.

Mark Kurlansky, *World Without Fish*. Workman Publishing, 2011.

Mark Kurlansky, *Cod: A Biography of a Fish that Changed the World*. New York, NY: Walker and Co., 1997.

Michael Pollan, *The Omnivore's Dilemma: A Natural History of Four Meals*. New York, NY: Penguin Press, 2006.

Michael Pollan, "An Animal's Place." *New York Times* Magazine, November 10, 2002.
http://www.nytimes.com/2002/11/10/magazine/10animal.html?pagewanted=print

L. Sneddon et al., 2003. "Do fishes have nociceptors? Evidence for the evolution of a vertebrate sensory system." Proceedings of the Royal Society, London, Series B 270: 1115–1121.

Casson Trenor, "Four Fish We Should Never Eat." AlterNet.com, March 30, 2011.
http://www.alternet.org/food/150407/4_fish_we_should_never_eat/
See also: http://www.sustainablesushi.net/

Judith S. Weis, *Do Fish Sleep?* Newark, NJ: Rutgers University Press, 2011.

WEBSITES

Center for Biological Diversity. http://www.biologicaldiversity.org

"World's Fish Catches Being Wasted as Animal Feed," Farm News from TerraDaily: News about Planet Earth, October 30, 2008.
http://www.terradaily.com/reports/World_Fish_Catches_Being_Wasted_As_Animal_Feed_999.html

Pew Memorial Trusts Marine conservation campaigns.
http://www.pewtrusts.org/our_work_detail.aspx?id=937

Video: *What to Eat: The Environmental Impacts of Our Food.* http://www.platetoplanet.org

CONTAMINATION

"Food safety concerns have been on the rise worldwide with increased globalization and several high-profile scandals, including in China in 2008, when tens of thousands of babies were sickened after companies added melamine to milk products, making them appear to have more protein than they did."[1]

Dioxins are the unintended consequence of the chemical revolution that ushered in the Age of Plastics. This era began in the nineteenth century with commercial applications for celluloid, a plant-based, acid-transformed material that, among its other uses, replaced elephant ivory in billiard balls. Bakelite, first synthesized in 1907 (the first completely synthetic material), outperforms celluloid: it keeps the shape into which it has been molded, despite successive applications of heat. Bakelite provides strength that is durable, lightweight, and inexpensive to produce (in contrast to steel), and therefore it found favor with the War Department for use in World War II weaponry. Battery casings made of Bakelite lie buried, intact but, thankfully, inert, in today's landfills.

Subsequent new materials and the processes to manufacture them would not prove as gentle on the environment. In the 1950s and '60s, households and businesses added new names to their vocabularies and our shopping lists: vinyl (PVCs), Saran Wrap, and Teflon—and in the wake of this upsurge in plastics, the dioxins arrived.

Dioxins are POPs (persistent organic pollutants). Along with eleven others chemical complexes, they comprise the so-called "dirty dozen"—all toxic, long lasting, environmental-polluting chemicals. Most POPs, like DDT (dichlorodiphenyl trichloroethane), are manufactured intentionally. The dioxins (poly-chlorinated dibenzo-p-dioxins) are the unintentional by-product of combustion, usually from industrial processes, like the uncontrolled incomplete burning of waste products, especially plastics.

When animals (human or otherwise) ingest dioxins, these poisons are stored in fat tissue rather than secreted, and there they will remain for a half-life of seven to eleven years,[2] able to cause damage to cells and metabolic processes in the form of cancer and other diseases. Developing embryos are especially susceptible to their toxic effects. To a lesser extent, breast milk from a mother with a significant body burden of dioxin proves harmful to her nursing infant.

An industrial accident in Seveso, Italy, in 1976 released a toxic cloud over a populated area. The immediate and long-term health of this population is being monitored, as well as that of children born after the accident. In 2004, dioxin made headlines in an infamous case of alleged intentional poisoning. The victim was Viktor Yushchenko, then the Ukrainian president. The dioxin he ingested did not prove fatal, but his face was seriously disfigured by chloracne, a condition caused by a form of dioxin, TCDD, found in Agent Orange and also in Love Canal.

Dioxins have natural sources (they are released as a result of forest fires and volcanoes), but the majority of these pollutants are man-made—released from industrial combustion, whether from some step in a manufacturing process, an industrial accident, or from improperly burned industrial waste. Whatever their source, dioxins are transported by the wind. In this haphazard way, dioxins cover the globe. They sink, insoluble in water, to the bottom of oceans. Landing on soil, they coat plants in fields where grazing animals forage. But unless one is grazing cattle near the charred fields of Chernobyl or Mount St. Helens, or immediately downwind of an illegal incinerator, it is unlikely that the concentration of dioxins will be significant or easily measurable. If dioxins ever became profitable or desirable, one's local Superfund site would be an ideal place to dig for them.

For humans, the main source of exposure to dioxins comes from our food, literally from the food our food ate before we ate it, which is a long way of saying "bioaccumulation." Poisonous chemicals accumulate as they are passed along, up the food chain of who eats who and what, with the ultimate predators (usually humans) receiving the full load of whatever has been eaten by all the organisms lower down the chain. Dioxin is stored in the fat cells of meat, dairy, and egg producers, fish and shellfish. Transformed by slaughter into human food, their dioxin load is transferred to us, for storage in the fat cells in our bodies, as the next critter up the line.[3]

How do dioxins get in animal feed? The problem, like agribusiness, is global in its size and complexity. Whether by accident or on purpose, borne of ignorance, sloppiness, or greed, mistakes have been and will continue to be made in the manufacture of animal feed—mistakes that traverse international boundaries and constitute a challenge to public health.

Dioxin gets into animal feed from a variety of sources worldwide. Dioxin-laced clays used in the manufacture of animal feeds are found in Japan, Spain, and the United States. In 1997, in the United States, increased levels of dioxin in eggs, chickens, and catfish were traced to a mined-clay product used in the production of animal feed as an anti-caking agent and an aid in the formation of pellets. There is speculation that dioxins in the clay were formed by prehistoric ash from forest or volcanic fires. Dioxin in clay was again identified as the contaminating agent in Austria and Germany in 1999, in 2004 in the Netherlands (forcing a recall of milk), and in Germany that same year when clay-contaminated potato peels forced the closure of several farms.

In 1998 toxic levels of dioxin found in German milk were traced to animal feed made from citrus pellets exported from Brazil. In 1999 illegal dumping of PCB industrial oil waste contaminated animal feed in Belgium, forcing a recall of eggs, poultry, and pork from several countries.

In 2003 waste from a bakery was found to have high dioxin levels, and was being used as animal feed.

In 2007 dangerous levels of dioxin were found in guar gum, a food additive manufactured in Switzerland from a plant grown in India and Pakistan and used to thicken various products from yoghurt to ketchup. The plant was contaminated with a pesticide (PCP) residue. The process to manufacture PCP created the dioxins, but because the thickener was a low-fat, plant-based product, regular testing for dioxin contamination was not done. The tainted product was sent to customers throughout Europe, Australia, Japan, and Turkey.

Discarded human food, dried with high dioxin content fuels contaminated Irish pork in 2008. In 2010 organic eggs were contaminated with dioxin made from Ukrainian corn. In Germany contaminated eggs were combined with clean eggs to make pasteurized liquid egg products, and then shipped to customers in United Kingdom. The "diluted" levels of dioxins were "not thought to be a risk to health."[4]

This brief list provides a glimpse into the web of international commerce involved in agribusiness that has gone industrial and global, both in terms of the supplies the farm industry purchases and the animal and plant products it sells. Two changes from the past increase the dioxin risk we face when eating animal products: more dioxins are produced by industry all the time, and more of them will find their way into the human food supply due to the nature of the closed system by which we recycle these toxins. Once in the system, the dioxin endures, "persists," whether in the contaminated feed consumed by a cow, or the slaughterhouse waste that once was part of that cow, consumed by another cow or pig or chicken or us. This is not like it used to be.

Animal feed for the traditional family farm was something homegrown and simple, rather than a trucked-in complex compound of pelletized materials, including animal fats from slaughterhouse waste. In a pre-plastics atmosphere, chickens scratched outdoors for bugs and a handful of corn probably grown in a nearby field; pigs ate table scraps and cows grazed a few acres of pasture. Today's industrialized agribusiness increases opportunities for dioxin contamination because of the global net that must be cast to gather the nutrients that go into feed, and the manufacturing processes that pelletize it, and the economic pressures to make it for less and sell it for more, following the capitalist mantra: buy low, sell high.

When animal agriculture is industrialized, it goes global almost by default because economies of scale favor the vertical organization of the global producer and threaten to put local producers out of business. Call it "walmartlogic." Animal husbandry for the small farmer or herder offers a slim profit margin but the hope of sustainability for water, land, and energy. The corporate farm multiplies the number of product units and lowers the cost per unit of production, be it an egg, lamb chop, or quart of milk. It is neither ecologically sustainable nor humane, but per unit of production, it is cheaper, if one discounts the likelihood of being poisoned by one's food.

"There are no factories that I know of that have existed for five hundred years. Yet there is land the world over that has been managed agriculturally for hundreds if not thousands of years. The industrial model seeks to control nature; the agrarian seeks to manage it."[5]

NOTES

1. Judy Dempsey, "Germans Fear Dioxin Has Contaminated Small Farms." *New York Times,* January 7, 2011.

2. WHO fact sheet #225, May 2010.

3. Food and Agricultural Association of the United Nations pamphlet, "Health hazards associated with animal feed: Manual of Good Practices for the Feed Industry."

4. http://www.ourfood.com/Dioxin.html

5. Peter Kaminsky, *The CAFO Reader: The Tragedy of Industrial Animal Factories.* Healdsburg, CA: Watershed Media, 2010, p. 312–313.

Farmaggedon 2011 South Korean government orders 9million animals culled because of Foot and Mouth disease. Pits were lined with plastic, and 90% of the 9million were buried alive.

FOOT-AND-MOUTH DISEASE

Sometimes the cure is worse than the disease. Sometimes the disease is more economic than biological. Such is the case with Foot-and-Mouth Disease (FMD). Unsanitary conditions encourage outbreaks. Yes, it is contagious, as easy to catch and pass along as the common cold, and like a cold or flu, is viral in origin. Yes, it hurts: painful blisters on the mouth and gums discourage eating, so weight loss is certain. When a dairy cow is infected, her milk production falls off while she is ill and may never regain its pre-disease levels. Additionally, she may become sterile. Quarantine measures isolate animals on farms where outbreaks occur to protect neighboring cattle from exposure to the virus, but the disease is not fatal. In a matter of weeks most all the animals that contract Foot-and-Mouth have recovered. Or they would have, had they not been slaughtered en masse, the healthy along with the sick.

What then explains the practice of culling, both the sick and the well, considering that humans are naturally immune and the flesh and milk of the recovered victims are safe for human consumption? The answer lies in profit margins and the desire to maintain consumer confidence in a brand name.

Let's unpack the assumptions that cling stubbornly to news of a Foot-and-Mouth outbreak. A mindset resembling a cross between mercy killing and frantic attempts to ward off the Black Death precedes the rush to cull an infected herd. Neither concern is justified. The motivation to cull stems strictly from economic factors. While the animals that contract Foot-and-Mouth could recover, the bottom line is a goner for those whose infected animals produce meat and milk for the market.

There is a vaccine, but that costs money, and must be administered before the animal gets sick. The vaccine is prepared on a "best guess" estimate of which strain of the virus will be the attacker in any given season. And truth be told, the farmer will be compensated for his loss, through private insurance or government subsidy, so farmers do the math: the cost of vaccines that may not be 100 percent effective; of feed and care while the animals recover; of loss of market share for lighter weight animals, sterile cows (no more use to a dairy farmer than a bull), lower milk production, and therefore profits, for the same amount of feed consumed.

The power of a brand name or a slogan lies in the confidence it inspires in consumers. The 1958 Edsel, for a host of reasons having nothing to do with how well the car functioned, demonstrates what lack of consumer confidence means. A country that can claim no Foot-and-Mouth has earned economic bragging rights, the psychological edge on the international market for its T-bone. "No FMD" is a reassuring slogan like "contented cows," "grass-fed beef," or "no MSG." Fundamentally, culling for Foot-and-Mouth is inspired by the same motivation to keep crazy cousin Dafka out of sight when the prospective in-laws visit.

As the Nazis found out, it is hard work to kill tens of thousands in a short time, and harder still to dispose of their bodies. In the old days, cattlemen dressed for a cull in rain slickers, rubber pants, and boots. They ringed the trench into which the cattle had been driven, and at a signal, uncradled their rifles and began shooting. The guns eventually drowned out the frightened bellows, and after a while, only the guns would be heard. Once all was quiet, quicklime was shaken atop the dead and dying, and earth shoveled over it all.

Today, protective suits give those who must do the killing the appearance of space invaders. The modern trench may be lined with plastic. On Korean pig farms, the cull protocol includes the administration of a drug to paralyze the animals before they are buried, semiconscious but alive. When, as it happens, supplies of the drug run out, the animals are just buried alive, their struggles rippling, but never breaking through, the surface of the soil.

Slaughterhouse Trenton
Sue Coe 06

LIVESTOCK PROTECTION COLLARS

The rancher, like the farmer, faces an unforgiving, uncertain profit margin. Losing a sheep or goat to disease or accident shows up in red on a balance sheet. A herd living on the open range is subject to the perils of weather and predation. Not much can be done about the weather, but the livestock protection collar, a predicide developed in the 1970s, is noteworthy both for its selectivity and its potential for environmental contamination. It is used without regulation in South Africa to kill black-backed jackal. In the United States, with EPA regulation, the predator of choice for the collar is the coyote.

The collar comes with two rubberized compartments, each filled with a liquid poison, sodium fluoroacetate, simply known by its catalog number, Compound 1080. Coyotes attacking an animal go for the throat, the same area covered by the collar when it is properly fitted. Teeth puncture the rubber container and the poison splashes into the coyote's mouth. The sheep or lamb will die quickly of suffocation, but hours later, so will the attacker. Collars have been registered for use in Texas, Montana, Wyoming, South Dakota, and New Mexico.

Coyotes did not evolve with sheep and goats. They have to learn to identify these domestic animals as potential prey. Coyotes normally hunt small mammals and birds (recall the animated Wile E. Coyote and the honking Road Runner), and are also opportunistic scavengers. Unlike the average fast food consumer, most predators, coyotes included, reject a supersized prey in preference to one that is smaller and weaker. The coyote that has learned to hunt sheep or goats will be more likely to target lambs and kids. Reflecting this fact, the collars come in both lamb and adult sizes, the smaller size being the one thus far approved for use in the United States.

The collar is misnamed; it does not protect livestock. To do that, it would need to provide the sheep with neck armor. Instead, the collar executes with "perfect justice" the predator who likes to pick on sheep or goats as a source of food. Better to call it the Eliminator. The collar acts, in effect, as a self-selected executioner for any predator that has learned to target sheep and goats. Its selectivity in this regard is a point in its favor over the use of indiscriminate leg hold traps and poison baits that will kill whatever creature comes along. However, there are potential environmental costs associated with the collar, and one can question whether, at twenty to twenty-five dollars, good for one use only, it is cost effective.

The poison comes dyed a bright shade of yellow or pink, to ease identification of a kill site and attendant soil contamination. Training in proper fitting, use, and inspection of pastureland is mandated, along with suggested ratios of pasture size to the number of collars thought practical. It is not practical to collar all the lambs and kids in a herd. Given the possibilities of ground contamination, and considerations of bang for buck, the collar is one more economic burden on the rancher, and an ecological burden on the land.

NOTES

Livestock Protection Company Collars website: http://www.livestockprotection.net

Factsheet May 2010. The Livestock Protection Collar, Wildlife Services, United States Department of Agriculture, Animal and Plant Health Inspection Service. http://www.aphis.usda.gov/wildlife_damage/

Dale Rollins, Texas Agricultural Extension Service, Wildlife Specialist, Texas Natural Wildlife, "The Livestock Protection Collar . . . for removing depredating coyotes: A search for perfect justice?" http://agrilife.org/texnatwildlife/coyotes/table-of-contents/

C. J. Brown, "Test of Compound 1080 from a Poison Collar on a Captive Vulture." *Vulture News*, vol. 29: 19–26.

R. Pollitzer, "Plague Studies: 10. Control and Prevention," *Pub Med Bull.* World Health Organization. 1953; 9 (4): 457–551.

A brief back-and-forth history of regulation and registration:
Sodium Fluoroacetate, the poison in the livestock protection collar, history of use, and how and why re-registration is requested.
first regulated 1947.
reviewed 1964 and 1971.
1972 cancelled.
1977 experimental use permitted to do risk assessment on benefit of toxic collars.
1981 EPA asked to reconsider 1972 decision.

1982 EPA agrees to reconsider.

1985 registration granted for toxic collar, transferred 1986 to Animal and Plant Health Inspection Service (APHIS) at USDA.

1989 all registrations cancelled, all pending applications denied by August 1990.

1995 decision made that product is eligible for re-registration, will not pose unreasonable risks to humans or environment providing used in accordance with the restrictions on product labeling.

EPA June 1995 R.E.D. (Reregistration Eligibility Decision).

2011 EPA is re-initiating and reconsidering refining the label of the product.

She dies unnoticed

Decompression - the chickens ear drums explode, and their lungs collapse

Sue Coe 11

DECOMPRESSION

In the 1870s, an unknown disease killed fifteen caisson workers engaged in the construction of the Eads Bridge, a cantilevered steel marvel spanning the Mississippi and connecting St. Louis, Missouri, to East St. Louis, Illinois. The bridge pushed the architectural envelope of its day, and not just for its graceful design or its reliance on steel as the primary building material. The Eads was among the first to build its foundations using caissons (think of an upside-down glass tumbler submerged in water, only much larger), sunk deep in the mud of the river bottom. Inside the caissons, with air pressure kept high enough to keep out water and mud, workers excavated to bedrock and lay the foundation for the piers, unaware that decompressing (returning to surface air pressure too quickly) would kill or injure them.

They called it caisson disease. It is extremely painful, particularly to the joints, which may be why it is also called "the bends," as victims bend and writhe to find a less painful way to hold their limbs. Deep sea divers who ascend to the surface too quickly may get the bends. The decompression forces bubbles of inert gases, i.e., nitrogen, into the bloodstream, skin, and joints.

Today, in Fort Smith Arkansas, a chicken packing company, OK Foods, is trying out decompression as a slaughtering method for its birds.[1] As this patent-pending process is described: ". . . the birds are placed in a sealed cylindrical chamber and the pressure in the chamber is reduced at a continuous rate to a target decompression pressure for a period of time until a state of death is obtained.

The process ruptures eardrums and collapses lungs as the gas bubbles lodge in the joints and brain. Young birds can withstand the decompression better than older ones and thus take longer to die, up to four minutes.

Why the interest in patenting such a process? Don't laugh, but studies of this method are ascribed to the search for a humane chicken slaughter method. Current industrial methods involve shackling, dunking in cold, salted, electrified water, designed to paralyze the muscles of the chickens' feather follicles in order to loosen their feathers and immobilize them on the assembly lines prior to slitting their throats. Alternatively, some processors use a gas chamber. The American Humane Association finds decompression more humane than either shocking or gassing, but the American Veterinary Medical Association doesn't. Neither do cities that once (but no longer) used the decompression method to destroy homeless, unwanted dogs and cats.

Postscript: June 14, 1874—a "test elephant" was urged to walk across the new Eads Bridge to convince the public the bridge was safe. The assumption then was that elephants could sense an unsound structure and would not walk on anything that could collapse. The elephant crossed with no problem, and the bridge stands to this day.

NOTES

1. Karen Davis, "Decompression: A New Way to Torture Chickens and Turkeys to Death," United Poultry Concerns, April 28, 2011. http://www.upc-online.org/slaughter/decompression/

Pigs Eaten Alive
by Maggots

Sue Coe 2010

THE PIG FARM AT LETY

The history of the labor camp turned pig farm in the Czech Republic village of Lety[1] is deceptively simple and politically complex: just prior to the German annexation of the Sudeten region in the late 1930s, the camp was one of hundreds built throughout the former kingdom of Bohemia to lock away those deemed unclean: unworthy of respectful treatment, those denied the protections of human rights. For the Lety camp, this meant "Gypsies," or more accurately, the itinerant Romany peoples. Once the Germans took over, Jews were rounded up as well. They were formed into gangs of slave labor, good only to be worked to death. In 1943, a typhus epidemic closed the Lety camp. Survivors were sent to die in the industrialized death camps of the Third Reich, where some were first tortured in so-called "experiments." After the war, on the camp's site, Germans in the region—those who supplied Hitler with an excuse to annex the Sudetenland—were "ethnically cleansed." Their bodies were added to Lety's mass grave. By the end of the war, approximately 126,000 Roma from Romania, Poland, Hungary, Germany, and France had died in either the slave labor camps or the purpose built death camps associated with the Holocaust. Hate crimes against the Roma continued after the war, much as they had before. The region was now a Soviet satellite. In the 1970s, atop this small, former killing field for humans, the Soviet government built an industrial-scale death camp, this time for hogs.

Today, the Roma want the pig farm moved; they want respect shown for those who suffered there and died. Presumably they want to remember, bring to light what was hidden or ignored for decades, and this is laudable. Not far away, on the site of another labor camp that held and killed many Roma, there is now a hotel. There has yet to be a move to tear down the hotel. Why is the pig farm more offensive than the hotel? The Roma believe pigs are unclean. Tourists are acceptable. But more to the point, the factory farm is a reminder of something the Roma are in two minds about—they would like the world to remember the terrible wrongs done to their loved ones, and they would like to ignore the fact that the Roma attitude toward pigs echoes the attitude of the Nazis and contemporary skinheads toward the Roma. In one twisted sense, the pig farm makes the best possible memorial to those who died; it is a living echo of the past, producing fresh death and suffering daily.

Moving the farm would answer the Roma's immediate needs, but it begs other questions: a new farm in some other location won't change living conditions for the pigs, or their ultimate fate. The Lety camp exchanged human torture for animal torture. What permits such torment and abuse to occur in the first place? A partial answer must include the practice of dividing living beings into Them and Us. This framing allows Us to hide Them, to ignore and forget Them. We hide Them from Us because we would rather not look too closely at the inequities—the ghettos, jails, factory farms, and slaughterhouses—where They are condemned to live and die.

NOTES

1. Gwendolyn Albert, "Pigs Out of Europe! Concentration Camps and Czech Pork," *Left Curve*, no. 23. http://www.leftcurve.org/LC23webPages/lc23toc.html

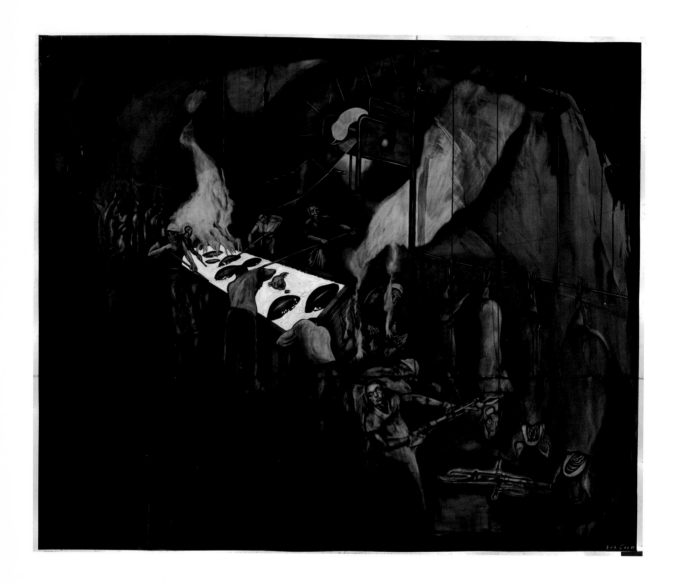

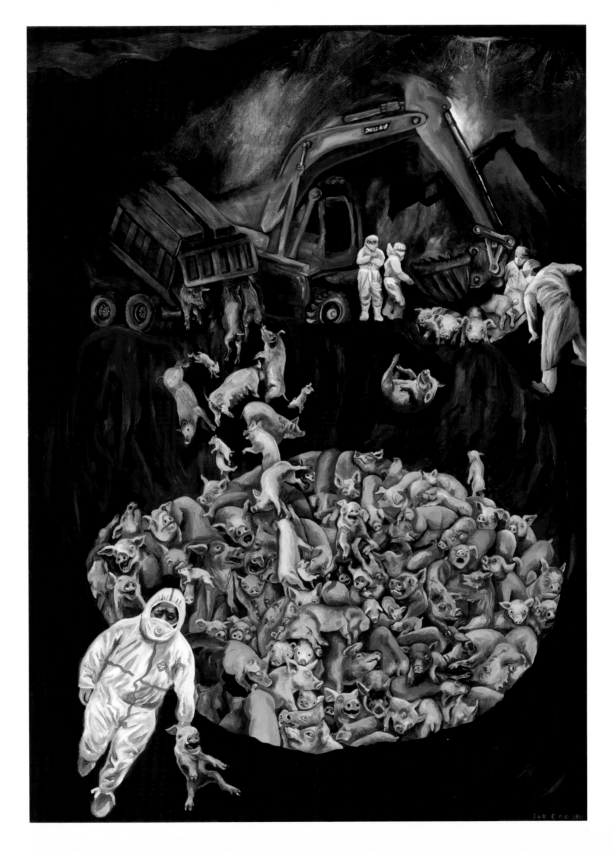

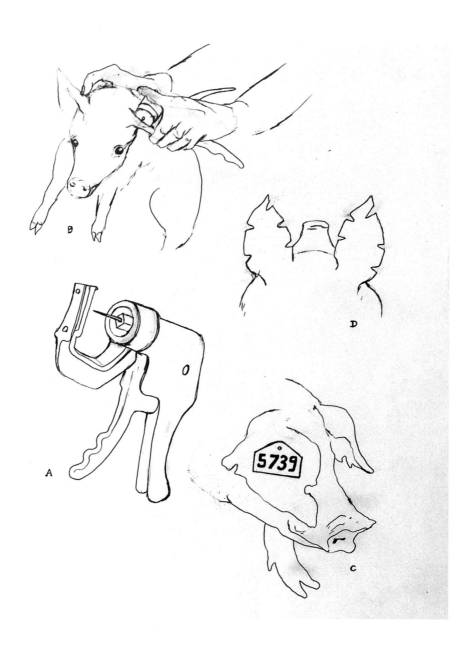

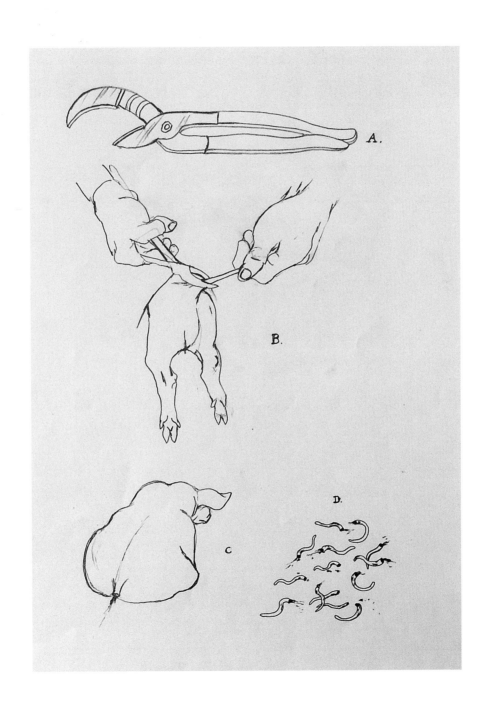

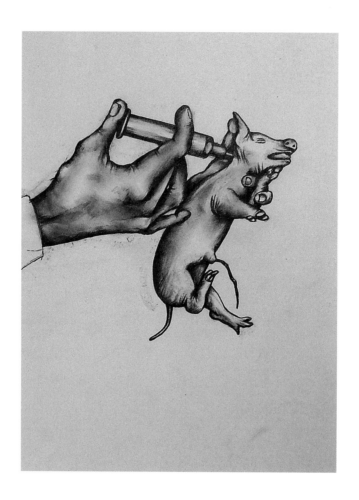

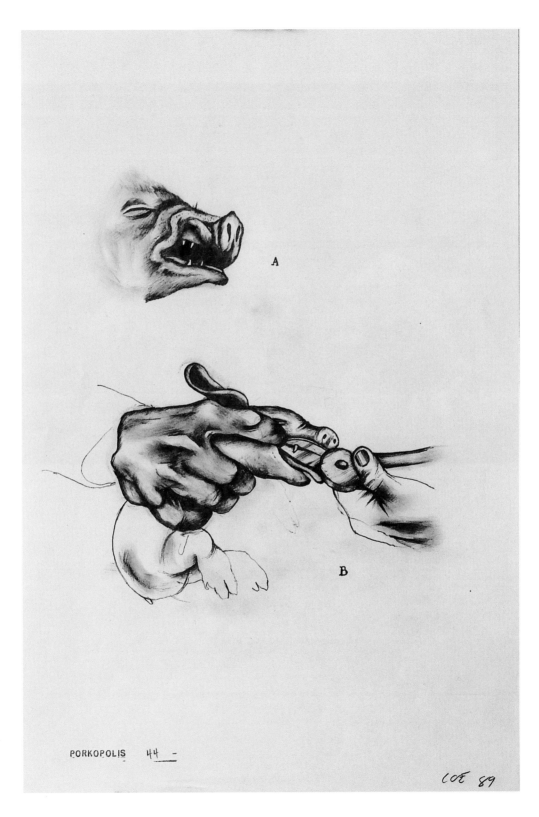

A

B

PORKOPOLIS 44 –

COE 89

THE PORTAL: A PARABLE

One night, on a distant planet many light years away, a portal opened to the underworld.

The planet was haunted, inhabited by all the ghosts of beings and entities that had been murdered for profit; they died such cruel deaths that they collectively willed themselves into a time of the past and future, where there was peace and beauty and where they could be safe. Those who died natural deaths went to a secret place, or even nowhere, a place that cannot be revealed at this time.

Seeing the portal, the ghosts tentatively moved over to it, as they were curious, and they peeked over the rift into the chasm. As there were trillions of ghosts in all forms, and the portal was small, they had to take it in turns to go to the edge and look down.

It was very dark, and a death mist hung over the place, so the ghost of starlight and the ghost fireflies offered to illuminate. The stench was unbearable, so the ghost of clean water offered to spray the area with a light rain, and the ghosts of clean air, tried their very best to diffuse the smell. Ghost trees stood up high on their root tips and used their leaves to circulate the breeze. The ghosts of flowers used their petals and sweet scent to try and mask the terrible smell.

As the ghosts were a loose democracy, they discussed amongst themselves which ghostly tribes would be allowed to look first and then report back.

It was decided that the ghosts who deserved to go first, the majority, were the farmed animals, who outnumbered any of the other ghosts, and who were still mostly babies when they died. Who had suffered the most barbarism, had no life, went insane behind bars and barbed wire, been beaten, punched, mutilated, genetically changed, whipped, chained, raped, branded, kicked, had their babies stolen to be murdered, and then had been eaten by creatures who were not even hungry. They deserved more knowledge as to why the world was the way it was.

The cows and calves were the most curious and excited, they galloped over to the brink, their large brown eyes watering at the fumes. They helped the smaller animals like the chickens, ducks, turkeys, and geese to see, letting them stand on their broad backs. The pigs were strangely nervous, they had enough ancient memory to know this would be bad, but still, they had to look as well. The goats and sheep would only go all at once, and as they had no leader, they waited for one to appear; they bleated quietly to themselves.

The cows and calves took one peek, and the cockerel called a warning, and then they all galloped back as a giant wave of light, as far away from the portal as they could run. The feathered ones would have stayed longer, but were obligated to leave when the cows did. Although they generally trusted the cows, there was some clucking and chirping and crowing that it was not fair.

The other ghosts waited patiently and watched the pigs carefully move forward on trembling trotters. The ghosts of mountaintops waited—they were used to waiting—the ghost rivers waited, those with fins waited, and the two-leggeds who had died in wars or prisons or of starvation, they waited too.

The pigs were frightened not so much by the stench or the heat, but by the noise emanating from the fissure: the deafening screaming and cursing, the clanging chains, gunfire, reverberating explosions that reminded them of when they had died in a slaughterhouse. The elephant and giraffe ghosts standing nearly as tall as the mountains could look over the heads of the ghostly crowd and watched the pigs with sympathy.

The chickens were brave, despite their frailty; they wanted to know and they followed the pigs. What they saw they tried to accurately remember to share with the others. Some pigs took notes, to set a good example for the piglets to be accurate. Some even made sketches. It may seem trivial now, for the pigs to have made notations of names they heard, or of a snatch of a phrase or gesture, but it was not their task to make sweeping conclusions about what this all meant, but rather to gather whatever information they could remember to tell the others.

Deep inside, down in the gloom along the steep chasm, was a kind of weird décor—hieroglyphics, cave paintings of corporate icons—scratched and smeared on the walls. Flat screens that depicted wealth and power that flickered on and off were embedded in the rock, along with logos and bar codes. The largest screen of all was for stock prices, and it went down into the bowels of the planet until it disappeared. There were ugly, grotesque creatures writhing at the bottom of the pit, feeding on the flesh and blood of each other. They could not conceal their putrescence, and some were stamped with the logos of corporations; they could not take their eyes off the changing prices—ever—they could never blink or close their eyes even for a second; they made terrible cries and curses, or mad giggles whenever the stock quotes changed. Wars and disasters made the most money, and they all competed to be in on the horror. If no disasters existed they would create them. They would clutch their wads of money sooner than push in the intestines and colons oozing from the gaping wounds they had inflicted on each other. Occasionally they would set up a chanting hymn that sounded like a scream; the words stated their deep-felt superiority: that they were on top of the pyramid, that everyone and everything else was there to be used, that capitalism was the real god that fed on life as disposable meat to be eaten or worked to death.

Those that were the strongest and had accumulated the most wealth rose to the top of the stinking heap, but the top kept changing, as they bludgeoned and stabbed each other and erected more and more ladders of bones and skulls to clamber over rotting corpses, and the ladders kept breaking. The stink rose from their defecations and urine and blood. Unlike the ghosts on the planet's surface who were composed of pure light, these creatures were fleshy and heavy, always feeding on each other and digesting, tearing at each other. Their smeared waste dried on the corporate icons, and then crumbled off. There was never a second when they were not fighting or killing and selling each other.

The pigs and chickens listened carefully, controlling their gag reflexes, trying to decipher the utterances coming from the mouth holes in the creatures' faces as they screamed at each other. The words most oft-repeated that the pigs could discern were Power, Control, Money, Profit, Enemy, Hedge Funds, War, Fear, Victory, Budget, Bond Ratings, Celebrity, Homeland, God, Lawsuit.

Bobbing at the top were the Royals, festooned with jewels and cloaks of animal bodies, until the weight of their gold crowns and viscous teeth pulled them under and they disappeared under the writhing mass.

Another corporate creature called JBS was adept at staying on the top, and because of diversified global protein production wealth and its expertise at slaughtering animals, it was busy slaughtering other corporate entities, as the non-human animals had ceased to exist. Flesh and blood were JBS's wealth, and it had a little helper called the USDA who had turned so many blind eyes that it was covered head-to-toe with dark glasses.

Bankers bobbed to the top, clutching bags of swag; they would sooner drown then let go of the gold, so they sank.

An entity called Murdoch was seemingly everywhere, trying to rule eternal night; he was the personification of cynicism—mummified, grey, and sinister—telling the phantom audience he was only giving them what they wanted: entertaining lies. His eyes sunk deep into his skull, his nails a foot long—he bred tabloids and TV stations, all glassy heads shouting to an audience without eyes or ears. He looked up at the pigs and promised them a world of blissful ignorance, if they would only hand him their minds. A fetid three-headed glove puppet was clinging to a Murdoch leg—the heads were called Beck and Limbaugh and Palin—and they kept fondling Murdoch's inner thigh, all the while gurgling confusion and spewing forth hatred from their hideous throats.

Palinhead was drenched in the blood of wild animals, which made the pigs and chickens cringe in fear.

One of the heads had a blackboard with signs on it, but the chalk was filthy, so no signs could be made out. The pigs knew only the puppets' names because their names and ratings were stamped on each forehead. Occasionally Murdoch would reach down his leg and crush a head, to make another appear: a Trump head, or a Roger Ailes head.

Sulfurous flames shot up, laden with radiation, and brought forth mutated generals who floated on armchairs. They had never fought wars personally, but liked to watch others die in video drone games on their flat screens and iWants. Their rows of medals proved too heavy for them to stay afloat for very long, and they sank back into the bubbling sewer.

The politicians stuck to the periphery, on the walls, drying out and going crispy and curling from the heat. They never rose very high, but maintained hopes of ascending by getting votes from those holding their noses and checkbooks. Money was bait, dangled in front of them by corporations—the Supreme Court judges, living in corporate sweaty armpits, facilitated even more wealth by changing the laws of the pit to benefit those on top.

It was a complex, always changing hierarchy and the pigs were confused, but it was not their task to understand the history of their extinction by these murderers, only to report back on what they had witnessed.

A group called Halliburton/XTO/Exxon wanted to frack the entire sewer—to descend deeper into the underworld than ever before, among the gaseous fumes. The well drillers were laden with poisonous chemicals and carried a Dick Cheney heart as their standard (that, one of the ghost pigs recognized with a sad shock, had been torn from her own body).

As fast as they fracked, they poisoned all the potential buyers, which made no sense at all to the observing pigs. The gas drillers were owned by the same entities as the oil drillers, who owned the nuclear power stations, yet they competed with each other to see who could get the last drops of fossil fuel or radiation to sell to those who died eons ago.

When the fumes and steam thinned so the pigs and chickens could see more clearly, an entity in a cloak called Cover Up blurred the view.

A politician, grinning forever, spotted the pigs gazing down from on high, backlit by a halo of starlight, and called up that he was Change that pigs like them could Believe in, and if they would only drop down a rope there would be a new beginning, one with no more ham and bacon. This politician clutched a Porcine Peace Prize which impressed the pigs very much, and they wondered what he was doing down there with the others. But then the pigs saw he was concealing by his shadow *Wars with No End*, and when he turned slightly to the right, they could see the back of him, and it was the front of a warmonger called George W. Bush. As the pigs turned their snouts from these conjoined twins, the two voices growled in a sinister reverberating echo that if the pigs did not vote for them . . . something much, much worse was waiting. As the pigs were dead already, they wondered what could be worse. The murderous entities would steal their imaginations? Control their thoughts?

When the gas frackers rose to the surface, simultaneously with the endlessly marrying, scandal-ridden Royals, they screamed, "Frack her cracks and get on with it," to the wedding party, and then sank down again.

The captain of the scientists, Descartes, floated around, trying to vivisect whomever he could get his scalpels into; he was swatted off by International Pork and Beef, which required entire carcasses. MacDonald's and Kentucky Fried Chicken were estimating the exploding population of flesh eaters and counting their profits, while being consumed themselves by pharmaceutical companies.

The surface writhed into ever-changing configurations, drenched in oil and sweat and other secretions; one moment it was Popes in lamé dresses and gold pointy shoes who spoke to a heavy gold cross and told the pit residents he was speaking on behalf of the One True God, and then in a wink of an eye up came the Mullahs who said they owned the only True God and that triggered them murdering each other over and over again, and then they sank back into the gloom. The pit creatures banked whichever god was the richest and changed their allegiances as fast as the ticker tape would allow. Sometimes they gazed up at the pigs and swore pigs would be worshipped as gods, if only they would lend a trotter.

Bloated Profit oil corporation slithered and floated around on the top nearly all of the time, and if floating at the top of a sewer was a measure of a success, then BP was the best: it dribbled oil out to Lobbyists who sucked it down. The oily body reflected the little light there was until its exploding rig legs lit the cavernous walls. This was one of the busiest of the entities, bribing and lying, covering up, manipulating politicians and governments, making billions of ghosts for billions of dollars; their motto was profit before life and they made sure that no life remained unsold. Transocean boasted of their safest year ever while gorging on the bodies of their employees. Attached to BP and ExxonMobil were millions of tiny shareholders, succubi, who had no eyes but mouths that could speak up to object, if only they had stopped feeding off the monster. They gurgled, their mouths full of blood and oil, that they had to pay their mortgages, they were doing it all for their children. But they were never sated, they wanted more and more. They drank in the oily secretions from every orifice and then rolled off to drink from each other. BP tried to throw up oil barrels, as piggery bribes, but the pigs had no use for it, as they had no corporeal bodies and could not drive.

The pigs had seen enough; they wept at this terrible view from the portal. The chickens dried their eyes with soft wing feathers and clucked and cheeped over the horror. It reminded them that science and logic and reason cannot change the unreasonable and irrational. The sight of these callous monsters brought forth feelings they had long since forgotten: helplessness, fear, misery.

How to report this to the innocent others, who had forgotten who had murdered them?

A hen was the elected president of all the ghosts. In her physical life, she was frail and grey, with wounded skin stretched taut over broken bones. She had lost her feathers and one eye, her beak had been severed, parts of her toes were missing: they remained gripping the steel bars when she was torn from her cage. But in her ghost life she was sleek; her feathers shone with the colors of the rainbow. And under her wing she had chicks. While she was alive, she saw them rendered worthless, but in this world they were cherished. Her beak was bright orange, and her eyes sparkled with wisdom and empathy.

The question was put: Why was this happening? Why did the portal open? Why did the animals now have the burden of memory? Would these monsters infect their spirits?

The ghost animals, trembling with fear, gathered around the hen to listen to her thoughts.

She spread her wings to shelter all the animals, and they calmed. Her wings grew enormous, larger than the universe, somehow embracing both the elephants and the tiniest butterfly. The hen said that the portal and all the monsters therein did not exist anymore, that they were but a shadow, a nightmare of eons past, that the monsters had no power to destroy a dream, that that was their delusion. Their greed and selfishness had prevented them from entering this world, they had sold tomorrow for the hell of their self-made present and so had lost their powers. The animals had imagined a different world, and although it was all in their imagination, some day it would become real.

She folded her wings back into her body with a soft rustling sound, and all the animals walked and swam and flew away from the portal without looking back.

sketchbook

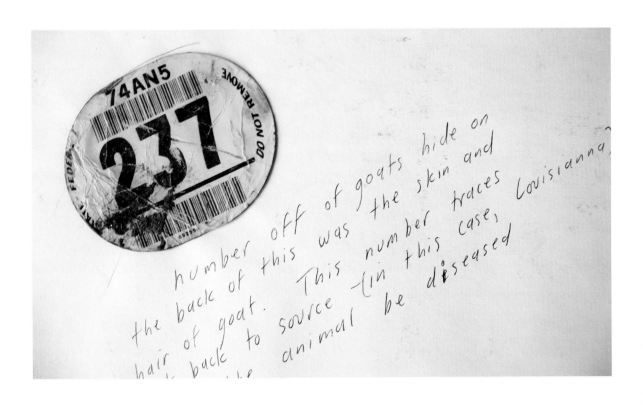

number off of goats hide on the back of this was the skin and hair of goat. This number traces back to source (in this case, Louisianna) the animal be diseased

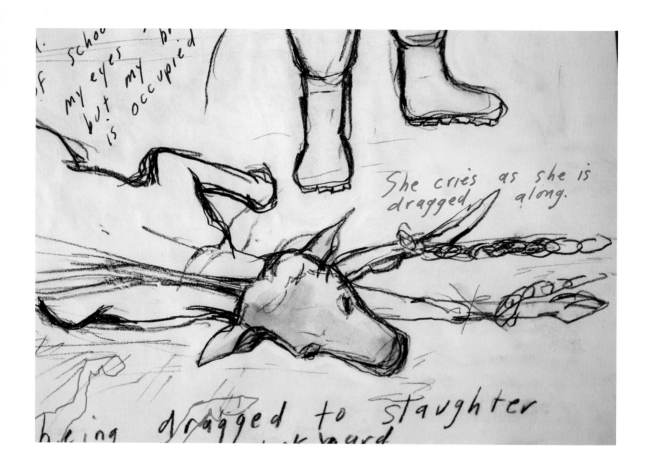

dragging goat out
of pen by one horn.

... water at stockyard
in St Paul - its Sunday - 95°
She struggles to get
up (I think her
back might be broke.
White froth is coming
out of her mouth
She makes one
last attempt, but
the movement
throws her head
back, which now
seems too heavy for
her neck, and
then she is still

dying calf
at stockyard.

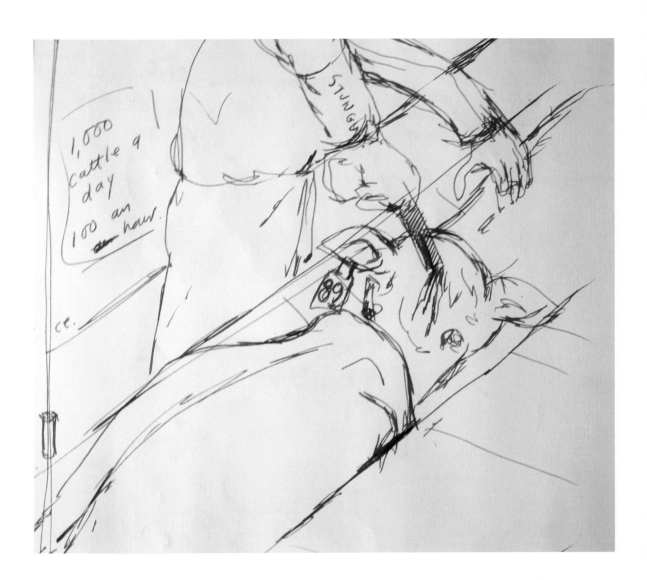

procedure is repeated. The floor is covered with blood, I can see my reflection in it. On the walls are saws, and knives, and different pullies.

One sheep is let in. She is white-with a blue brand on her side, and black feet. The door closes. She runs around the kill floor. The workers seem to forget her, they are not know in the killing pen, but over by the skinning table having a conversation, in whispers. The forman comes over and says, not to put any of their faces in my pictures. The sheep waits, her hooves and legs are covered with blood. The door opens again, and 2 sheep are pushed in- the outside worker doesn't know the killing has stopped. The sheep start to bleat. (bleet?) The sheep terrible soft sounds. Piteous cries. The sound falls out of the thick air, as though it never was.

Steaming water from the hoses, runs the old blood away down the drain. And the killing starts again. I'm glad Santiago is there, although I barely know him. I feel responsible for putting him in this situation. I see, what is going on

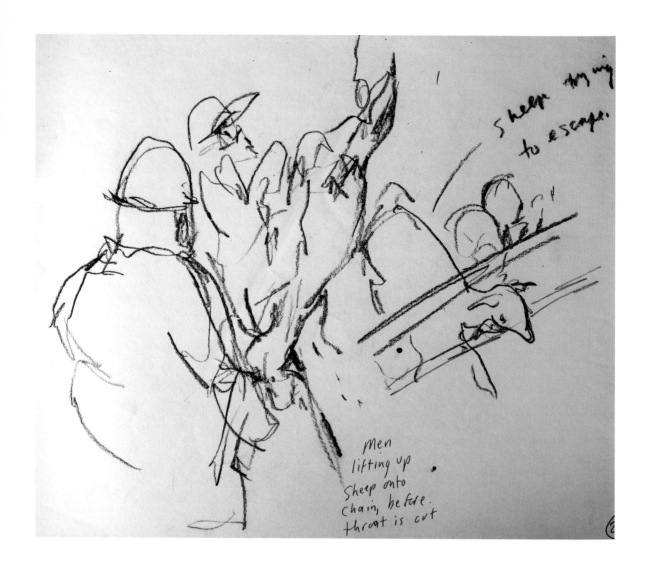

decapitated cow.

Ken taking off hooves

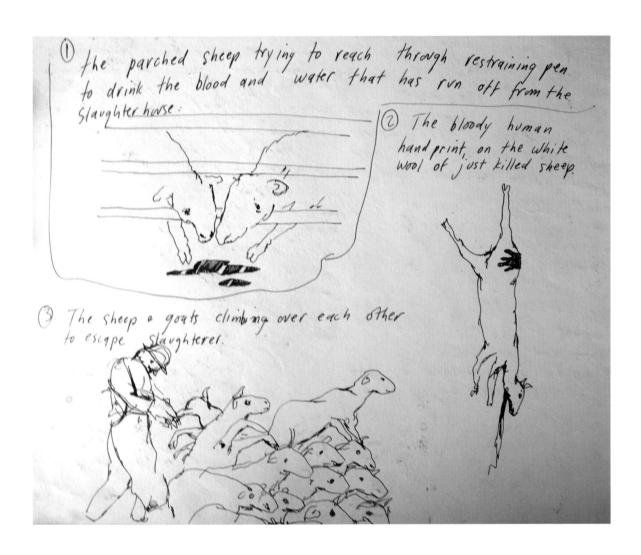

① the parched sheep trying to reach through restraining pen to drink the blood and water that has run off from the Slaughter house.

② The bloody human hand print, on the white wool of just killed sheep.

③ The sheep & goats climbing over each other to escape slaughterer.

They work, its repetative motion, a hundred veals, hung and skinned.

I look at the skinners han there is something wrong, I look more closely and each finger has been severed at the joint. He has only stumps and thumbs

WITH SPECIAL THANKS TO:

Karen Davis

Stephen Eisenman

Kim Stallwood

Dr. Thomas Brody

David Craig

Sue Coe was born in Liverpool, England and grew up next to a slaughterhouse. She studied at the Royal College of Art in London and left for New York in 1972. Early in her career, she was featured in almost every issue of the groundbreaking magazine *Raw*, and has since contributed illustrations to *The New York Times*, *The New Yorker*, *The Nation*, *Entertainment Weekly*, *Time*, *Details*, *The Village Voice*, *Newsweek*, *Rolling Stone*, *Esquire* and *Mother Jones*, among other publications. She is widely regarded as one of the best and most scathing artists of her time. Her paintings have been exhibited in galleries and museums around the world, including New York's Museum of Modern Art. Her previous books include *Dead Meat*, *How to Commit Suicide in South Africa*, *X*, and *Pit's Letter*.

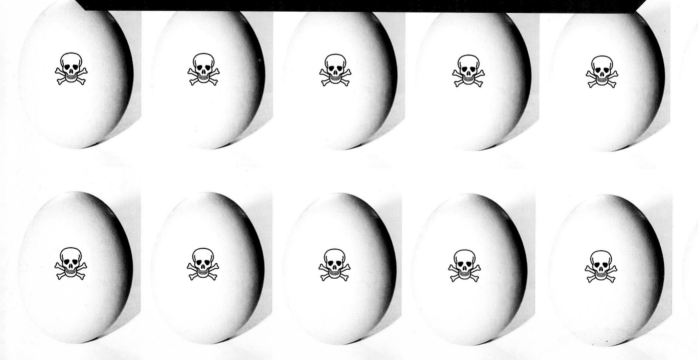